***Dr.*** most highly endorsed authors of all time!

**Dr. Kaplan** and his books have been highly acclaimed and endorsed by such people as President Donald Trump, Jack Canfield, Tom McMillen, Brian Tracy, Marla Maples, Kathy Coover, Norman Vincent Peale, Mark Victor Hansen, Earl Mindell, Harold Kushner, Mike Kryzyzewski, Johnny Damon, Lee Haney, Duane Clemmons, Ken Blanchard, Patch Adams, Les Brown, Wally "Famous" Amos, Rudy Ruettiger, Hall of Famers: Gary Carter, Barry Larkin, Billy Cunningham, Richie Guerin *and many, many more!*

**The 1 Minute Motivator:**
**A Book of Motivational Quotes and Life Philosophies**
***by Dr. Eric Kaplan***

# Praise for Dr. Kaplan & His Minute Motivators

Dr. Kaplan changes the world "1 Minute" at a time. His new book will inspire you and motivate you and is a must-read.

**Dr Thomas Caputo**
Disc Centers of America
Lawrenceville, GA

Motivation in "1 Minute" increments. So easy and so powerful. Anyone can read his words and reap the benefits. It's even great for young adults.

**Michael Taylor, DC**
Disc Centers of America
Chicago, IL

Dr Kaplan is not only a brilliant physician who wrote a brilliant book, but he is a brilliant CEO in the world of business as well. Wherever he speaks across the globe, I make it a point to attend, and I devour anything that he writes. This amazing book will change your life as it has changed mine. Dr Kaplan inspires me every day of my life as he has for the last 25 years that I've known him personally and professionally.

**Dr. Richard Lohr**
Disc Centers of America
Decatur, IL

I have read the "The 1 Minute Motivator" twenty times. A sure bestseller.

**Dr. Melinda Keller**
Brooklyn New York

Dr. Kaplan packs a lifetime of success into his book, "The 1 Minute Motivator." This book will keep you in a positive frame of mind. Thanks again, Dr. Kaplan!

**Dr. Tim Kamerman**
Chiropractic Care Clinic
Searcy, AR

If you have ever had the privilege to talk with Dr. Kaplan one-on-one for "1 Minute," you will understand what I mean. His laser focus way of communication gets straight to the point. What others take twenty minutes to teach, he does in a minute or less. Get this book and hold on; your life will never be the same.

**Dr. C. Nick Viscusi**
Disc Centers of Vacaville, CA and Napa, CA

Dr. Kaplan is a force of energy that is striving to change the world one person at a time. His new book will inspire you "1 Minute" at a time. Anything he writes is a delight to read.

**Steven P. Thain, DC**
Disc Centers of America
Bellevue, WA

Anyone who wants to lead a happier, more successful life needs to read Dr. Kaplan's new book. I will give it to my staff. It will empower any reader.

**Dr. Raymond Bates**
Disc Centers of America
Franklin, TN

Wow. This book is a simple, straightforward answer to the question, "How do I make myself and everyone around me better?" It is a must-share with all the people who work for me and are important to me. Thank you, Dr. Kaplan, for your dedication and commitment helping others achieve success and a happy, rewarding life.

**Michael Putman, DC, CFMP, CErg**
Twin Creeks Health

This book is a classic, I love sharing the "1 Minute" philosophies of life with my family. A must-read to anyone who wants to grow. I'm excited to share this book with patients and friends. Thank you, Dr. Kaplan, for a fun and entertaining read.

**Dr. Reza Nikpour**
Annandale, VA

Dr Kaplan helps all to see that it only takes "1 Minute" to make a life changing positive effect in your life and the lives of all you meet.
Remember that each minute is precious, as that what life is made of!

**Dr Forrest Edwards, DC, DABCO**

Dr. Kaplan's books are so motivational, I read them over and over, and I share them with my patients. This book provides the empirical formulas to success. He allows you to imagine the power of "1 Minute."

**Dr. Dan Weymouth, DC**
Neighborhood Wellness
San Leandro, CA

Dr Kaplan is a one of kind man who changes the world "1 Minute" and one person at a time. I'm confident that his new book will inspire you daily.

**Dr Idan Snapir DDS**
The Dental Smile Center
Los Angeles, CA

Anyone who wants to lead a happier, more successful life needs to read Dr. Kaplan's new book. I will give it to my staff. It will empower any reader. Dr Kaplan is a force of nature. Thank you for everything you do.

**Dr. Brigitte Rozenberg**
Founder of Mineralgia natural pain-relief cream

It has been said, "The road to success is always under construction." Dr Kaplan's book provides the empirical formulas to success, not only in business, but in life!

**Dr Ted Wedell**
Kirkland Chiropractic and Massage
Kirkland, WA

Dr. Kaplan's books are so motivational, I read them over and over. Imagine the power of "1 Minute."

**Dr. James Dietrick, DC, CCEP**
Contra Costa Disc Centers

Dr. Kaplan is the master at condensing time to achieve phenomenal results. If you need guidance on how to go from bad to good, good to better, better to best than this book is for you. It's life changing!

**Dr. Paul Hoyal, DC**
Disc Centers of America
Kansas City MO

Dr. Kaplan changes the world "1 Minute" at a time. His new book will inspire you daily.

**Thomas Ferrigno, DC**
Bay Area Disc Centers

Dr. Kaplan's books are so motivational, I read them again and again! Thank you for making me a better doctor "1 Minute at a time!

**Dr. Cameron Roe**
Disc Centers of America
Anna TX

This is one of the most motivational reads I've read in a long time. Time is not our enemy; it is our friend. Dr. Kaplan teaches us the value of time his "1 Minute" approach sets the standard of excellence.

**Dr. Graham W. Kern, D.C**
Lakeland Disc Center

The search is over! Finally the magic pill of "plug and play" motivation exists today. Much more than a booster shot of motivation, Dr. Kaplan's game plan to success is the simplest, easiest, most concise and direct strategy to bring out the BEST in each one of us. My only regret is I didn't have access to it years ago. *The 5 Minute Motivator* will serve as the master plan in laying our personal course to our #1 desire to achieve, to become and to WIN!

**Dr. Perry Bard,** CEO Concierge Coaches
Author of *The Doctor Success Spotlight Book*

As a pro athlete I sought out the best in training, nutrition, and healing and Dr. Kaplan was always the first one I would call. His life experience and formal training as a doctor made him a trusted resource for guidance throughout my career. He exposed me to non-invasive, drug free, state of the art healing that repaired me and prepared me for a career in sports wellness after 10 years in the NFL. A life-long friend, mentor, and practitioner, his lessons of life are shared in his book. His book sacks the competition, literally. It's a must read and I'll share it with my players and friends.

**Duane Clemons,** Vikings, Defensive Captain of
Kansas City Chiefs and Cincinnati Bengals,1996-2006

*The 5 Minute Motivator* offers a practical, unique approach to experience greater success and happiness. This book will help you appreciate the blessings in your life.

**Marci Shimoff,** #1 New York Times Best-Selling Author of
*Love for No Reason* and *Happy for No Reason*

This wonderful book shows you how to become a totally positive person every day and accomplish more than you ever thought possible "5 Minutes" at a time.

**Brian Tracy,** Professional Speaker, Best-Selling Author of more than 40 books, Business/Life Coach, Sales Trainer CEO of Brian Tracy International™

*The 5 Minute Motivator* lays out a simple and powerful program for achieving your goals and dreams and triumphing over the inevitable setbacks and challenges we all experience.

**Pamela Yellen,** Author of the New York Times Best-Seller
*Bank On Yourself*

Dr. Eric Kaplan's, *The 5 Minute Motivator* is the complete guide for positive transformation! Brilliantly simple and simply brilliant. I encourage you make this book your daily helping of positivity and watch your life transform into the beautiful destiny you were meant to live.

**Peggy McColl,** New York Times Best-Selling Author of
*Your Destiny Switch*

Dr. Kaplan continues to educate and motivate—300 seconds at a time. His new book, The 5 Minute Motivator provides a magical stairway to a life changing experience. Success is about knowing who you are, believing in yourself and applying the principles, techniques and systems, he has so carefully provided the reader in his new book. If you are looking to be the best you can be, this book will change your life 5 minutes at a time.

**Dr. Fabrizio Mancini,** President, Parker University and Parker Seminars, Author of *The Power of Self-Healing*

The tools and insights that Dr. Kaplan shares in his book, *The 5 Minute Motivator,* are instrumental for anyone hoping to achieve their life's goals. This book will teach you how to make things happen and get results in life, "5 minutes" at a time. If you are looking for positive change in your life, this book of enlightening materials should be a must for your library.

**Dr. Joe Rubino,** Best-Selling Author of 9 books, including
*31 Ways to Champion Children to Develop High Self-Esteem*

*The 5 Minute Motivator* is a slam dunk for anyone who wants to reboot their life. Dr. Kaplan's prescriptions are time honored—the power of the mind to change our lives. As the Bible and Dr. Kaplan teach us, "What you sow in your thoughts, will determine what you reap in life". This book is a must read.

**Tom McMillen,** Former Congressman and Chairman of
President's Council on Sports and Physical Fitness and
11-year NBA veteran

Is it possible to invest 300 seconds with a book and receive a life-changing idea that can redirect your life? Such a book is Dr. Eric Kaplan's, *The 5 Minute Motivator*. As the co-founder of a dynamic growing company, thousands of associates and customers look to me for direction and motivation. So who motivates the motivator? Dr. Kaplan motivates me.

**Kathy Coover,** Co-Founder, Executive Vice President
Isagenix International LLC

No life or business is free from adversity. How we deal with that adversity will ultimately determine our success as business leaders and individuals. Eric Kaplan has faced adversity head on and grown to become a recognized leader in health, wellness and chiropractic medicine. His latest book is a must read for anyone dealing with the day to day challenges of running a business or a family. He presents a new way to look at the world which will become a powerful tool for anyone trying to harness the impact of change.

**William Meyer,** Chairman Meyer Jabara Hotels,
Chairman of the Kravis Center for the Performing Arts,
Vice Chairman of The Quantum Foundation,
Recipient of the Haym Salomon Award,
Serves on the Board of Overseers of the
School of Social Policy and Practice at the
University of Pennsylvania

Dr. Kaplan's book will add "Time to your Life and Life to your Time." He is one among those in the quest for immortality and in "5 Minutes" he explains the power of telomeres and their ability to turn back the clock. He touches the mental, spiritual and the physical keys to living a healthy happy life, one minute at a time; a must read for anyone who wants to be healthy, live longer and enjoy their time on this planet.

**Dr. Bill Andrews,** PhD, Telomere Scientist
Founder and President, Sierra Sciences

*The 5 Minute Motivator* offers advice to help the reader construct a life of success and happiness.

**Tony Hsieh,** New York Times Best-Selling Author of
*Delivering Happiness* and CEO of Zappos.com, Inc.

Dr. Kaplan Talks the Talk and Walks the Walk, literally. After being 100% paralyzed and making a miraculous recovery, he understands what it takes to win. His will and positive mental attitude are displayed in the pages of his new book, *The 5 Minute Motivator*. As a professional athlete, I understand the inner winner we all must reach for to succeed in life. Dr. Kaplan's book Awakens the Winner in us all. This book is a must read. I highly recommend it,

**Mark McNulty,** PGA Tour Professional, winner of 58 events, including
5 Majors, Senior PGA Championship, Senior British Open Championship,
US Senior Open, Senior Players Championship

I love Dr. Eric Kaplan's new book, *The 5 Minute Motivator*, for its simplicity and yet profound impact on one's life. It is truly an inspirational book for many

**Ping Li,** Best-Selling Author of
*Awakening: Fulfilling Your Soul's Purpose on Earth*

A powerful guide to living life well, *The 5 Minute Motivator* proves that time invested in our truest purpose is indeed time well-spent.

**Christine Louise Hohlbaum,** Best-Selling Author of
*The Power of Slow: 101 Ways to Save Time in Our 24/7 World*

Dr. Kaplan's new book, *The 5 Minute Motivator* will help you gain a renewed and vivid appreciation of life, minute by minute. The book offers a "tool kit" that will infuse your brain with a new sense of aliveness and possibility.

**Anat Baniel,** Clinical Psychologist and Best-Selling Author of
*Move Into Life* and *Kids Beyond Limits*

Dr. Kaplan's book provides not only the empirical formula to winning and success, but he provides you with a map, "5 Minutes" at a time. His skills as a teacher, educator, and motivator are second to none. This book is must read for anyone looking to reach their full potential.

**Tom Ness,** Golf Professional, Author Golf Digest,
Recognized by Golf Digest as one of the
Top 50 golf instructors in the United States

Dr. Kaplan has written another life-changing book. *The 5 Minute Motivator* is a powerful and comprehensive guide to success and happiness that anyone at any age can experience. His book will help you build the life of love and happiness "300 Seconds" at a time. Thank you. Eric, for this important, life-changing book."If you want to experience inner fulfillment on a whole new level, read this book."

**Dr. Stuart Hoffman,** Amazon #1 Best-Selling Author of *I AM a Lovable ME!*

As an author, teacher and businesswomen, I will incorporate your lessons into daily ideas for living. I found your book uplifting and motivating. Your book is a gift that keeps on giving.

**Catherine MacDonald,** #1 Amazon Best-Selling Author of *The Way*

Dr. Kaplan has done it again—he motivates, inspires and entertains the reader throughout the entire book. This book is simply awesome. It's loaded with good values and lessons that every person should instill in their lives.

**Jacki Baskow,** CEO Baskow and Associates

What does it take to engage all your senses in a journey to discover your richest, most fulfilling life? According to author Dr. Eric Kaplan, it only takes 5 minutes! The deceptively simple premise—and sheer genius—of *The 5-Minute Motivator* is that miracles can happen by thinking and focusing differently for only 5 minutes a day. Using this inspiring book as your daily guide to those transformative moments will become a habit that you will never want to break.

**Dr. Christine Ranck,** Amazon #1 Best-Selling Co-Author of *Ignite the Genius Within*

As a professional golfer I understand what it takes to win—on and off the golf course. Dr. Kaplan has written another life-changing book that can show you the way to heath and happiness. He provides the reader with a powerful and comprehensive program that anyone can employ in their life regardless or their occupation. If you want to experience happiness and success at a whole new level, read this book. It will be the best "5 Minutes" you will ever invest in yourself.

**Dana Quigley,** PGA Golf Professional, winner of 29 events, 2005 Champions Tour, Player of The Year 2005

Dr. Eric Kaplan's, *The 5 Minute Motivator* shows us that the fulfillment which we so eagerly seek is actually just a few steps away. Through incredibly simple exercises, Dr. Kaplan helps us realize that we can achieve what we dream, inspire others to do the same, and that abundance already exists in each of our lives. It's up to us to recognize it. Pick up this book whenever you have a few spare minutes and allow it to replenish your positivity and reactivate your drive for life.

**Dr. Carmen Harra,** Clinical psychologist, intuitive counselor, and Best-Selling Author of *Everyday Karma and Wholeliness*

It is said that 'a people without a vision perish.' In *The 5 Minute Motivator*, Dr. Eric Kaplan takes you on an incredible journey where he unveils your inner gifts and unravels hidden mysteries to enable you to think with a winning mind and experience the dreams you've long desired.

**Ken Lang,** Author of *Walking Among the Dead*

*The 5 Minute Motivator* is a book for everyone who wishes to live their dream, inspire their children, and touch the lives of all who they know. If you wish to change your life and elicit the greatness within, then *The 5 Minute Motivator* by Dr. Eric Kaplan is the book to launch your success with. Every parent should share the wisdom in this book with the people they value most—their children. I loved my experience in reading this book!

**Dr. Ted Brooks**, Ph.D., MS., Nutrition
Isagenix Millionaire

Dr. Kaplan has certainly hit the nail on the head with his latest work, *The 5 Minute Motivator*. There are times in life when we need to be reminded of our strengths and that it's okay to reach for our goals in life regardless of our age. I would recommend this book to everyone, young and old, who wants to get more out of their circumstances in life.

**Dr. Ken Simpson,** DC, 2009 IsaBody Challenge Grand Prize Winner

Dr. Kaplan is someone for whom I have tremendous respect and admiration. As Mrs. United States 2005 and a cosmetic dentist, I see everyday how lives are transformed for the better based simply by how someone feels about themselves. Dr. Kaplan clearly has a gift that aids people in finding that place where life takes on a much brighter rainbow and beautiful outlook.

**Dr. Chiann Fan Gibson,** Mrs. United States 2005

Dr. Kaplan's book is more than highly motivational. It shows you how to simply and elegantly remove mental toxins, naturally. It's mandatory reading for anyone who wants to live a healthy, happy life.

**Beth Greer,** Best-Selling Author of
*Super Natural Home and Environmental Health Consultant*

If you are looking for a shot of inspiration read, *The 5 Minute Motivator* is a must read book. Dr. Eric Kaplan offers great tips to keep us on top of "the game of life."

**Caroline Sutherland,** Best-Selling Author of
*The Body Knows… How to Stay Young*

Dr. Kaplan offers his readers the opportunity to convert dreams into goals, change goals into plans, and live the life they've always wanted. He then delivers on his promise by offering practical advice, powerful stories, and needed inspiration… all in 5-minute bite-size pieces.

**Joshua Becker,** Author of #1 Best-Selling book, *Simplify*

As a firm believer in the power of believing in oneself, I was overjoyed to read a success story in which a small amount of time set aside every day, as little as 5 minutes, can command worlds of success. As proud as I am to endorse this book, I am even more gratified to know that its message will help and inspire others.

**Michelle Franklin,** Award-winning fantasy and romance author
Creator of *The Haanta Series*

*The 5 Minute Motivator* inspires anyone and everyone to be better—"5 Minutes" at a time. His words elegantly and spiritually compel the reader to look at the blessings of living, laughing, loving, and learning. A fun and powerful read.

**Anna Maria Prezio,** Author of #1 Best-Selling book
*Confessions of a Feng Shui Ghost-Buster*

*The 5 Minute Motivator* might be an understatement. This is a 5-minute life changer! While each snippet requires only 5 minutes to read, they contain a day's worth of digestion. There is so much power in each story and the quotations are inspiring and thoughtful. A great way to start each day that all rolls into an abundant life! How cool is that!

**Carl Bozeman,** Amazon Best-Selling Author of
*On Being God - Beyond Your Life's Purpose*

In the game of life, there is no playbook to winning better than Dr. Kaplan's new book, *The 5 Minute Motivator*. This book will take you on an adventure to success, 300 seconds at a time, I will share this book my staff, my friends, and my family. I know it will change and enhance their lives as much as it has mine.

**Carlos Becerra,** CEO North America Medical

I am lucky in that I interact with Dr. Eric Kaplan frequently and am always amazed by his clear and most helpful insights about how to deal in a positive way with life's many problems. Don't miss the opportunity to learn from his approach to healthy living. This book gets to the point—clear, precise, direct. If you want to reach your potential as a person this book is the empirical guide. A must read.

**Joseph Littenberg,** Senior Partner Lerner, David, Littenberg, Krumholz, and Mentlik, Recognized As the Best IP Counselor

*The 5 Minute Motivator* is a must read for any leader. Just setting aside 5 minutes per day for personal growth can be life-altering. Many pearls of wisdom are jammed-packed in this book with most of them told in parable stories which are memorable. Well worth the price of admission, I highly recommend that you also take a ride on this book adventure.

**Sam Santiago,** PMP, Amazon Best-Selling Author of
*The Official Book of Innovation*

Dr. Kaplan's book proves that in life you should never, ever, Give Up On Love. His book is more than highly motivational, it is inspirational. In an interval of only "5 Minutes" he helps the reader remove mental barriers that exist in life, in a natural and positive manner. I would consider this book essential reading for anyone who wants to live a healthy, happier, and more loving life. It is simple to understand and elegantly written. This book can help transform anyone, enabling them to reach their potential and fulfill their dreams.

**Tim Carroll,** Best-Selling Author of *Don't Ever Give Up On Love*

Our teachers and parents repeatedly told us the "keys to success." They said, "Stay focused! Concentrate! Play to your strengths!" Dr. Kaplan's, *The 5 Minute Motivator* teaches you how to VISUALIZE your success and confidently unlock your natural potential. The old phrases will now have new meaning because *The 5 Minute Motivator* shows you how to comfortably make these concepts part of your way of life and stay one step ahead of the competition!

**Ira Sherman,** Managing Partner, Chaikin, Sherman, Cammarata and Siegel, P.C., Past Pres., D.C. Trial Lawyers Ass'n.

# THE 1 MINUTE MOTIVATOR

DR. ERIC KAPLAN

# *I*ntroduction

Friends, I said in my fourth book *The 5 Minute Motivator,* "Success is based on attitude, and attitude can be altered by time." We are all born with an equal inheritance of approximately 700,000 hours. One of the great differences between life and death, is that life offers us a choice, while death offers a mystery. We have a choice of how we live these 700,000 hours and we can choose the quality of our existence on this journey of life. Many people live their lives in a whirlpool, marred by confusion, and absent of direction on their quest to succeed. Man and woman were born to succeed. It's the goal of this small book to continually activate endorphins by turning your basic coffee break into a mini-motivational break.

I have always considered myself a student of life; a motivator, educator, a philosopher on life and success. Many of the quotes in this book I have used in lectures, heard from my father, or received from my partner and muse, Dr. Perry Bard. Dr. Bard who I've lectured with for years, is a best-selling author and kept a book, called the "Red Book, of Life and Practice Principles", that he has shared amongst our many clients.

I challenge you to improve your life. Fact is it will only take "One Minute" Yes " One Minute", One Thought, One Gesture, One Idea, One good deed, One goal, One Friend, One smile, One laugh, One moment, may change your day, May change your life. Thirty Nine years ago, in "One Minute", I changed my life in two words, " I Do". My wife Bonnie of 39 years, my best friend, my muse, altered my life and the life of my family. I am a blessed man to know it took only two words and "One Minute" to change my life, to change my destiny.

Now it is your turn. Your turn to turn minutes in hours, hours into days, days into weeks, week into months, months into years and years into memories. However you must seize the moment, the minute, here, now. The world is full of opportunities waiting to be seized and as you've seen, new ones turn up every day. The key to most of these opportunities is taking action—action fueled by desire and complemented by energy. I challenge you to take action now. I challenge you to spend "**1 Minute**" a day, every day.

I challenge you to decide every day to be the best you can be. Remember, the key is to not change the world, but to change yourself.

In his best-selling book, *The Four Agreements*, author Don Miguel Ruiz writes: "to be the best you, you can be". This is my ultimate goal, to be the best me that I can be. And this is what I wish for you as well – to be the very best you that you can be.

I want to give special thanks to all my friends and family and especially my sons Jason & Michael and their lovely wives Stephanie & Jessica Kaplan. And to Allison Holland, soon to be Mrs. Allison Sladek, who was my designer and editor on this project, I could not have completed this book without her dedication to myself and Concierge Coaches.

I hope you enjoy this book. I dedicate this book to the two most influential people in my professional life - two people that love and support me in spite of myself. My wife of 39 and 1/2 years Bonnie Kaplan. And I especially want to thank my friend, my partner, my muse, my brother from another mother, Dr. Perry Bard. Dr. Bard teaches "success leaves clues." Well, he has now been in my life 32 years. I owe him my love and gratitude - he was my gift from God. And a very special thanks to Dr. Bard's amazing wife, Laura. Thank you for allowing him to work so hard, and for being a part of my family.

*Love you, Bonnie & Love you, Perry*

Lastly this book is written in memory of my father and mother, Mike and Elsie Kaplan, who believed in me more then I believed in myself.

*Thanks, Mom.*
*Thanks, Dad...*

# CHAPTER 1
## *Awakening Your Talents*

Benjamin Franklin wrote, "Do you value life? Then waste not time, for that is the stuff of which life is made." The value of anything that you obtain or accomplish can be determined by how much of your time, or your life, that you spent to acquire it. The amount of yourself that you use up in achieving the goals that are important to you is a critical factor to consider, even before you begin. Only by discovering your innate strengths and developing and exploiting them to their highest degree can you utilize yourself to get the greatest amount of satisfaction and enjoyment from everything you do. In this book the "One-Minute Motivator", I have gathered thoughts and sayings I have used during my entire life. Imagine, One Minute, 60 Seconds per day, could alter your conscious and your subconscious mind and activate your Superconscious to take you places you've always dreamed of. It only takes One Minute a day, to set a goal, state an affirmation, call a loved one, hug a friend. The One-Minute Motivator, will hopefully awaken your talents and desires in One Minute a day. Deciding what you want to do, what you can do well, and what can give you the highest rewards for your efforts is the starting point in getting the best out of yourself. *I ask you today to dedicate a few minutes of your time to bettering yourself.*

**Strategic Planning**

Having worked on Wall Street, I was brought in by many companies to do strategic planning. When I do strategic planning for corporations, I begin with the premise that the whole purpose of the exercise is to reorganize and reallocate people and resources to increase the rate of return on equity, or capital invested in the business. When Perry and I look at your business, we look at it in the same format, getting the most for your money with the greatest return. We do this by emphasizing some areas and de-emphasizing others, by allocating more resources to areas with higher potential return and by taking resources away from those areas that represent lower potential returns. By developing or promoting newer and better products and services and by discontinuing those products and services that are less profitable, the practice and all your staff can channel their energy and resources to maximize the office returns.

Now in our seminars, we want you to be the CEO, of your business, do this you must look at yourself as a leader and you must make strong business decisions. It is not always easy doing personal strategic planning, the first thing you want to think about is increasing your personal "return on energy," rather than return on equity. You need to realize that the most essential and valuable thing that you have to bring to your life and to your work is your ability to think, to act, and to get results. You're earning ability—which is a function of your education, knowledge, experience and talents—is your human capital, or your equity. And the way you use it will largely determine the quality and quantity of your rewards, both material and psychological, both tangible and intangible.

**Define Your Values**

This first part of personal strategic planning is called "values clarification." You ask yourself, "What values and virtues do I most admire and wish to practice in my life?" If you wanted to discover your strengths in the work world, first you would define your values as they apply to employment. The values that companies settle upon would be similar to the values that you organize your work life around. Often, both companies and individuals will choose values such as integrity, quality, respect for others, service, profitability, innovation, entrepreneurship, market leadership, and so on. For example, General Electric, as one of its values, is determined to be either first or second in quality and market share with any product that it offers. If it cannot achieve a first- or second-place position, it will make every effort to grow into it, or it will leave the market entirely.

4

In a similar vein, you could use those values to define your position with regard to your work. You could decide to plan your work life around the values of quality, excellence, service, profitability, and innovation. There are dozens of values that you can pick from, but whichever you choose, and the order of priority you place on your choices, will determine your approach to your work.

For example, you might say, "I'm an outstanding person, business person, leader, teacher, lawyer, Doctor, well-organized, hardworking, thoroughly prepared, positive, enthusiastic, and intensely focused on serving my patients better than anyone else can." With this as your mission statement, you have a series of organizing principles that you can use to guide your career choices, your personal- and professional-development activities, and your work schedule for each day. This mission statement also tells you the kind of person that you're going to be in your interactions with the people whose satisfaction will determine your career success. A clear mission statement also is a definition of the areas in which you intend to become stronger in order to achieve your goals.

**Define Your Goals**

Remember: Your goal is to identify your strengths so that you can deploy yourself in such a way as to increase your personal return on energy. One of the best mental techniques that you can use to accomplish this is to see yourself as a "bundle of resources" that can be applied in a variety of directions to achieve a variety of objectives. As a bundle of resources, the amount of time and energy that you have is limited; therefore, your time and energy must be put to their highest and best use. Stand back and imagine that you're looking at yourself objectively, as if through the eyes of another person, and you're thinking about how you could apply yourself to bring about the best results. See yourself as your own employer or boss. What could you do to maximize the output of which you're capable, and where could you do it?

Once you have defined your values and written out your mission statement, the next step is to do what is called a "situational analysis." Sometimes we call it a "performance audit." This is the process of analyzing yourself thoroughly before you begin setting specific goals and planning certain activities. You begin your performance audit by asking yourself some key questions.

One of those questions should be, "What are my marketable skills?" Think about it. What can you do for which someone else will pay you? What can you do particularly well? What can you do better than others? What have you done particularly well in the past?

A wage or a salary is merely an amount of money that is paid to purchase a certain quality and quantity of labor or output. The results that you're able to get by applying your strengths and your energies largely determine your rewards in life. If you wish to increase the quality and quantity of your rewards, you have to increase your ability to achieve more and better results. It's very simple.

Earl Nightingale said that the amount you're paid will be determined by three things: (1) the work you do, (2) how well you do that work, and (3) the difficulty of replacing you.

The laws of supply and demand also affect the labor market, of which you are a part. Employers or customers will always seek the very most for the very least. That means that you'll always be paid the very least that is necessary to prevent you from moving to another organization. Abraham Lincoln said that the only security a person can have is the ability to do a job uncommonly well.

The height of your income will be determined largely by how well you do your job and the difficulty of replacing you. In areas where workers can be replaced easily, the workers are paid only the minimum amount necessary to keep them. In increasing your return on energy, one of your objectives is to become so good in your chosen field that the cost of replacing you is extremely high. This is the way to assure that you will always be paid well because no one can get the kind of results that you can get for the amount that you charge, or the amount that you're paid (which are the same).

## Take Control

In reality, you're the president of your own personal-services corporation. You're completely in charge of production, quality control, training and development, marketing, finance, and promotion. Thinking of yourself passively, as being employed and, therefore, subject to the dictates of someone else, can be fatal to your long-term success. On the other hand, seeing yourself as self-employed forces you to see that you also are self-responsible and self-determining, that everything that happens to you happens because of your conduct and your behavior. You're in the driver's seat. You're behind the steering wheel of your life. It's up to you to decide how to utilize your talents and abilities in such a way as to bring you the very highest return on investment of your time and energy. No one else is going to do it for you. You're the boss. Others can help you, guide you, direct you, channel you, point you in the right direction and even give you opportunities, but in the final analysis, no one can make the critical decisions that will determine your future and your fortune.

## Define Your Strengths

Here are four questions that you need to ask yourself on a regular basis:

(1) "What do I most enjoy doing?"
(2) "How would I describe my ideal job?"
(3) "If I could have any job at all, anywhere, what would it be?"
(4) "If I won a million dollars in the lottery and I had to pick a job to work at indefinitely, what would I choose to do with my time?"

In uncovering your strengths, ask yourself, "What are my unique talents and abilities?" What have you been good at in the past? What things do you do easily that seem to be difficult for other people? In what areas of work do you seem to get the best results, and do you derive the most pleasure from? The answers to those questions all are indications of how you might deploy yourself to increase your return on energy invested.

As a result of your genetic structure, your education, your experiences, your background, your interests and proclivities, you're a unique and rare combination of talents and abilities. You can be extremely good at something. You're responsible for finding out what that something is and then throwing your whole heart into it, without reservation or holdback. Only when you discover what you really enjoy doing and then commit yourself to it wholeheartedly do you begin to feel really alive and fully engaged in life.

**Find Clarity**

Look at your current job and current abilities, and ask yourself, "Where do I want to be in three to five years?" What kind of work do you want to be doing? What kind of people do you want to be working with? What level of responsibility do you desire? What kind of money do you want to be earning? What part of the country do you want to be living in?

Let your imagination flow freely for a while. Imagine that there are no limitations on what you can do or be, or where you can do it or be it. Imagine that all options are open to you.

Look at your work and at your life in general today, and ask yourself, "What kind of people do I admire the most and want to be like?" Who do you know, or know about, who is doing the kind of work that you want to do and living the kind of life that you want to live? What changes would you have to make in your life to be like that person? Remember: Whatever anyone has done, someone else can do as well. You'll never be exactly the same as another person, but you don't need to be. You can use the successes and achievements of other people as examples and guidelines to help you decide where you want to arrive at the end of your particular journey, but you can be unique and different and successful in your own way.

Harold Geneen, the former CEO of ITT and one of the most powerful business executives in American history, always used to say, "Start with the goal and work back." So decide where you want to end up somewhere down the road, and then plan back to the present day to determine what you're going to have to do to get there. If you can make an honest assessment of your strengths and weaknesses, your threats and vulnerabilities, your areas of potential opportunity and the areas that might be holding you back, you're in a perfect position to begin looking forward to the future, to decide where you want to go and what you want to achieve.

**Be a Leader**

Finally, in personal strategic planning, the aim is always to achieve leadership in your chosen market niche. Business leaders have the authority to determine the area of excellence in their business. Analogously, on a personal level, you can choose the thing at which you're going to become absolutely excellent and achieve extraordinary results. So in what areas are you going to work to achieve results that are far beyond what the average person could be expected to accomplish?

What can you—and only you—do that, if done well, will make an extraordinary difference in your life? What can you do now, or can you learn to do in the future, that will give you the biggest payoff for the amount of time that you invest in it?

Remember: You were put on this earth with a special combination of talents and abilities that make you different from anyone who has ever lived. Whatever you're doing today, it's nowhere near what you're really capable of doing. The key to a happy and prosperous life is for you to regularly evaluate your strengths and weaknesses, to become very good in the areas you most enjoy, and then to throw your whole heart into what you're doing.

# CHAPTER 2
## *How One Minute Per Day Can Change Your Life*

Life is based on numbers: the seconds in a minute, the minutes in an hour, hours in a day, days in a week, weeks in a month, months in a year, and years in a life. The human body consists of approximately one trillion cells, which work 24 hours a day, 7 days a week, 365 days a year, never taking a vacation, let alone a minute off. When you stop to consider that the human body is perfect—that a heart beats an average of 72 times per minute, which is approximately 100,000 times per day, over 700,000 times per week, almost 3 million times per month, and over 34 million times per year—and never takes a minute off—you realize that our life is dictated by time.

We need to utilize time efficiently to experience all life has to offer. Life is like a combination lock, only with more numbers. If you select the right numbers in the right sequence, you can unlock the treasure chest of health, happiness, and success. In a short time, you can be the locksmith of your destiny. It takes just minutes of focus to change your psychology, alter your physiology, and transform you into the person that you were born to be.

The only way to break a bad habit is simply to drop it. What we need to do is create healthy, happy, and positive habits. By reading positive thoughts and reflecting on your life, the good in your life a minimum of once a day, will provide the power that can literally transform your destiny.

Imagine if success could be obtained by maintaining a positive attitude, a positive philosophy. Sounds simple, it isn't, but it's doable. Walt Disney said, "Your imagination creates your reality." Close your eyes. Look into your subconscious, your inner eye. What do you see? Like an architect, you must create the blueprint of your life. Imagine you could be anywhere you wished—on an island, in the mountains, maybe even at sea. Transport yourself wherever you wish. Smell the air. Feel the sun and the wind. Hear the  birds. See yourself smiling, at peace, and happy. Picture yourself as you want to be. Now, I ask you: How did you get to this place? You put yourself there through your imagination. Visualization will create reality. With this realization, you have learned the first key to unlocking your inner dreams—your imagination will create your reality.

## *How to Set One-Minute Goals...*

Plan your goals and work with setting goals with you family and business associates. The key is to describe to them briefly and clearly your plan and objectives. Show people what good performance looks like. There are three ways in life to lead…

# 1. By Example.
# 2. By Example.
# 3. By Example.

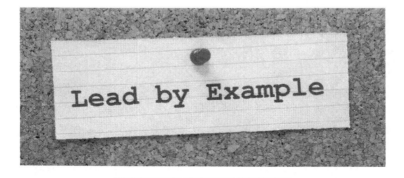

Lead by Example

Have your family or business associates write out each of their goals, with due dates.

***Remember, a goal without a plan, is simply a wish!***

- Take **1 Minute** a day to review with them their most important goals for each day, which takes only "**1 Minute**" to do.

- Encourage everyone to take **1 Minute** to look at what they're doing, and see if their behavior matches their goals.

- If it doesn't, encourage them to re-think what they're doing so they can realize their goals!

## *Give One-Minute Compliments*

- Compliment, and inspire people daily.

- Let people know what they do right, and be specific!

- Tell people how good you feel about what they did right, and how it helps.

- Pause for a moment to allow people time to feel good about what they've done.

- Encourage them to do more of the same.

- Make it clear you have confidence in them and support their success.

# CHAPTER 3
## *100 One-Minute Motivators*

# MINUTE MOTIVATOR #1

"More gold has been mined from the thoughts of men than has been taken from the earth. So dust off the cobwebs and use all those great ideas you have!"

*Now, spend the next one minute meditating and motivating yourself.*

## MINUTE MOTIVATOR #2

# "Free advice is the kind that costs you nothing… unless you act upon it."

*Now, spend the next one minute meditating and motivating yourself.*

# MINUTE MOTIVATOR #3

# "The road to success is always under construction."

*Now, spend the next one minute meditating and motivating yourself.*

# MINUTE MOTIVATOR #4

# "Even a clock that doesn't work is right twice a day."

*Now, spend the next one minute meditating and motivating yourself.*

## MINUTE MOTIVATOR #5

# "The only difference between possible and impossible, is two letters: I and M"

*Now, spend the next one minute meditating and motivating yourself.*

# MINUTE MOTIVATOR #6

It's important to focus on one thing at a time. Even in Ancient Chinese civilizations they understood this.
Consider this quote from Confucius:

"The man who chases two rabbits catches neither."

*Now, spend the next one minute meditating and motivating yourself.*

# MINUTE MOTIVATOR #7

# "Sometimes I think the surest sign that intelligent life exists elsewhere in the universe, is that none of it has tried to contact us."

*Now, spend the next one minute meditating and motivating yourself.*

## MINUTE MOTIVATOR #8

# "The best way to predict your future is to create it!"

# "CREATE YOUR FUTURE."

*Now, spend the next one minute meditating and motivating yourself.*

## MINUTE MOTIVATOR #9

"Before you criticize someone,
you should walk a mile
in their shoes…
That way, when you criticize
them, you are a mile away from
them and you have their shoes."

*Now, spend the next one minute meditating and motivating yourself.*

# MINUTE MOTIVATOR #10

# "When you point a finger at someone, remember, you have three fingers pointing back at yourself."

*Now, spend the next one minute meditating and motivating yourself.*

# MINUTE MOTIVATOR #11

# "Average is the best of the worst, the worst of the best."

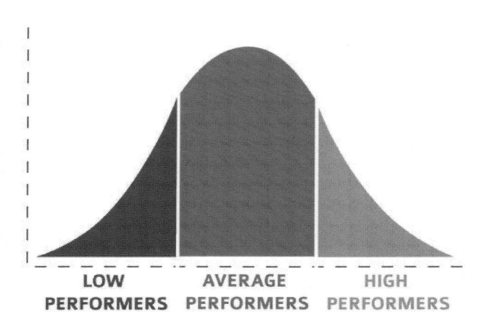

**LOW
PERFORMERS**   **AVERAGE
PERFORMERS**   **HIGH
PERFORMERS**

*Now, spend the next one minute meditating and motivating yourself.*

# MINUTE MOTIVATOR #12

# "If you think you are too small to make a difference, you have never been bitten by a mosquito!"

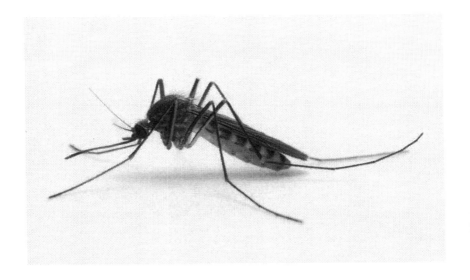

*Now, spend the next one minute meditating and motivating yourself.*

# MINUTE MOTIVATOR #13

# "Success comes in cans; failure in can'ts."

*Now, spend the next one minute meditating and motivating yourself.*

# MINUTE MOTIVATOR #14

## "The difference between an optimist and a pessimist is that an optimist thinks this is the best possible world. A pessimist fears that this is true."

*Now, spend the next one minute meditating and motivating yourself.*

# MINUTE MOTIVATOR #15

# "If at first you don't succeed, then skydiving definitely isn't for you!"

*Now, spend the next one minute meditating and motivating yourself.*

# MINUTE MOTIVATOR #16

"A foolish man tells a woman to stop talking, but a wise man tells her that her mouth is extremely beautiful when her lips are closed."

*Now, spend the next one minute meditating and motivating yourself.*

# MINUTE MOTIVATOR #17

# "Never be afraid to try something new. Remember, amateurs built the ark. Professionals built the Titanic."

*Now, spend the next one minute meditating and motivating yourself.*

# MINUTE MOTIVATOR #18

# "The latest new dance craze is called, "The Politician." It's two steps forward, one step backward, and then a side step."

*Now, spend the next one minute meditating and motivating yourself.*

# MINUTE MOTIVATOR #19

# "You have two choices: you can always be happy, or you can always be right."

*Now, spend the next one minute meditating and motivating yourself.*

# MINUTE MOTIVATOR #20

# "If you can't see the bright side of life, polish the dull side."

*Now, spend the next one minute meditating and motivating yourself.*

# MINUTE MOTIVATOR #21

My favorite saying: "A positive attitude may not solve all your problems, but it will annoy enough people to make it worth the effort!"

*Now, spend the next one minute meditating and motivating yourself.*

# MINUTE MOTIVATOR #22

"It's all about your attitude…
some people complain because
there are thorns on roses, while
others praise thorns for having
roses among them."

*Now, spend the next one minute meditating and motivating yourself.*

# MINUTE MOTIVATOR #23

# "A kiss is just a pleasant reminder that two heads are better than one."

*Now, spend the next one minute meditating and motivating yourself.*

# MINUTE MOTIVATOR #24

# "How things look on the outside of us depends on how things are on the inside of us"

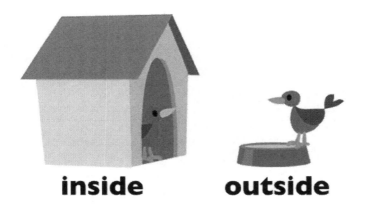

**inside**          **outside**

*Now, spend the next one minute meditating and motivating yourself.*

# MINUTE MOTIVATOR #25

# "If you are facing in the right direction, all you have to do is keep on walking in order to reach your dreams."

*Now, spend the next one minute meditating and motivating yourself.*

# MINUTE MOTIVATOR #26

# "It's not hard to make decisions when you know what your values are."

*Now, spend the next one minute meditating and motivating yourself.*

# MINUTE MOTIVATOR #27

# "Everyone is gifted… but some people never open their package!"

*Now, spend the next one minute meditating and motivating yourself.*

# MINUTE MOTIVATOR #28

# "There is no elevator to success. You have to take the stairs."

*Now, spend the next one minute meditating and motivating yourself.*

# MINUTE MOTIVATOR #29

# "The greatest oak was once a little nut that held its ground!"

*Now, spend the next one minute meditating and motivating yourself.*

## MINUTE MOTIVATOR #30

# "When your dreams turn to dust, vacuum! Start fresh—dream on!"

*Now, spend the next one minute meditating and motivating yourself.*

# MINUTE MOTIVATOR #31

# "The best angle from which to approach any problem is the try-angle."

*Now, spend the next one minute meditating and motivating yourself.*

# MINUTE MOTIVATOR #32

# "Life's problems wouldn't be called "hurdles" if there weren't a way to get over them."

*Now, spend the next one minute meditating and motivating yourself.*

# MINUTE MOTIVATOR #33

"Nobody trips over mountains. It is the small pebble that causes you to stumble. Pass all the pebbles in your path and you will find you have crossed the mountain."

*Now, spend the next one minute meditating and motivating yourself.*

# MINUTE MOTIVATOR #34

# "It's not who you are that keeps you back, it's who you think you're not. So, start believing in yourself!"

*Now, spend the next one minute meditating and motivating yourself.*

# MINUTE MOTIVATOR #35

"Though no one can go back and make a brand new start, anyone can start from now and make a brand new ending."

*Now, spend the next one minute meditating and motivating yourself.*

# MINUTE MOTIVATOR #36

# "You can't change the wind, so change your sails."

*Now, spend the next one minute meditating and motivating yourself.*

## MINUTE MOTIVATOR #37

# "I've learned that I should have told my mom and dad that I love and appreciate them more often than I did."

*Now, spend the next one minute meditating and motivating yourself.*

# MINUTE MOTIVATOR #38

# "I have learned that to ignore the facts, does not change the facts."

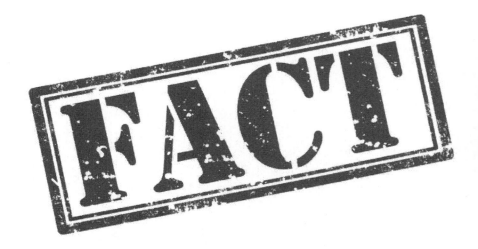

*Now, spend the next one minute meditating and motivating yourself.*

## MINUTE MOTIVATOR #39

"It's those small daily happenings that make life so spectacular. So, start enjoying those little things in life - often it's the little things that make the biggest difference."

*Now, spend the next one minute meditating and motivating yourself.*

# MINUTE MOTIVATOR #40

# "Everyone you meet deserves to be greeted with a smile. It makes his or her day, and mine too!"

*Now, spend the next one minute meditating and motivating yourself.*

## MINUTE MOTIVATOR #41

# "The easiest way for me to grow as a person is to make sure that I surround myself with people who are smarter than me!"

*Now, spend the next one minute meditating and motivating yourself.*

## MINUTE MOTIVATOR #42

# "I've learned one very interesting thing about money… it doesn't buy class."

*Now, spend the next one minute meditating and motivating yourself.*

# MINUTE MOTIVATOR #43

"No matter how serious your life requires you to be, everyone needs a friend to act goofy with. It brings you back down to earth again."

*Now, spend the next one minute meditating and motivating yourself.*

## MINUTE MOTIVATOR #44

# "Opportunity is always knocking."

*Now, spend the next one minute meditating and motivating yourself.*

# MINUTE MOTIVATOR #45

# "Your best friends are those that bring out the best in you."

*Now, spend the next one minute meditating and motivating yourself.*

# MINUTE MOTIVATOR #46

# "Life is tough, but I'm tougher!"

*Now, spend the next one minute meditating and motivating yourself.*

## MINUTE MOTIVATOR #47

# "When you harbor bitterness, happiness will dock elsewhere."

*Now, spend the next one minute meditating and motivating yourself.*

# MINUTE MOTIVATOR #48

# "Everyone wants to live on top of the mountain, but all the happiness and growth occurs while you're climbing it."

*Now, spend the next one minute meditating and motivating yourself.*

# MINUTE MOTIVATOR #49

# "A smile is an inexpensive way to improve your looks."

*Now, spend the next one minute meditating and motivating yourself.*

# MINUTE MOTIVATOR #50

# "The vitamin of friendship is B-1."

*Now, spend the next one minute meditating and motivating yourself.*

# MINUTE MOTIVATOR #51

# "Did you know that opportunities are never lost? That's because someone will always take the ones you miss!"

*Now, spend the next one minute meditating and motivating yourself.*

## MINUTE MOTIVATOR #52

# "The greatest pleasure in life is doing what people say you cannot do."

# Feel the fear and do it anyway

*Now, spend the next one minute meditating and motivating yourself.*

# MINUTE MOTIVATOR #53

"The funny thing about life is, if you refuse to accept anything but the best - you very often get it."

xaviereten

*Now, spend the next one minute meditating and motivating yourself.*

## MINUTE MOTIVATOR #54

# "There are no mistakes in life, only lessons."

*Now, spend the next one minute meditating and motivating yourself.*

## MINUTE MOTIVATOR #55

# "Solid advice: If you always tell the truth, you never have to remember what you say!"

# PLEASE DON'T LIE

*Now, spend the next one minute meditating and motivating yourself.*

## MINUTE MOTIVATOR #56

# "Always laugh when you can. It is cheapest medicine."

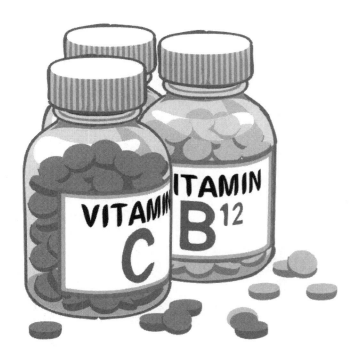

*Now, spend the next one minute meditating and motivating yourself.*

# MINUTE MOTIVATOR #57

# "If you could have everything, where would you put it?"

*Now, spend the next one minute meditating and motivating yourself.*

## MINUTE MOTIVATOR #58

# "Borrow money from a pessimist…

# They don't expect it back."

*Now, spend the next one minute meditating and motivating yourself.*

# MINUTE MOTIVATOR #59

# "The road to success is dotted with many tempting parking places."

*Now, spend the next one minute meditating and motivating yourself.*

## MINUTE MOTIVATOR #60

# "There is no telling how many miles you will have to run while chasing a dream."

*Now, spend the next one minute meditating and motivating yourself.*

# MINUTE MOTIVATOR #61

# "No one is perfect... that's why pencils have erasers."

*Now, spend the next one minute meditating and motivating yourself.*

## MINUTE MOTIVATOR #62

# "Great dancers aren't great because of their technique; they are great because of their passion."

*Now, spend the next one minute meditating and motivating yourself.*

# MINUTE MOTIVATOR #63

# "Volunteers are not paid; not because they are worthless, but because they are priceless."

*Now, spend the next one minute meditating and motivating yourself.*

# MINUTE MOTIVATOR #64

# "A society grows great when old men plant trees whose shade they know they shall never sit in."

*Now, spend the next one minute meditating and motivating yourself.*

# MINUTE MOTIVATOR #65

"Time goes by so fast; people go in and out of your life. You must never miss the opportunity to tell these people how much they mean to you."

*Now, spend the next one minute meditating and motivating yourself.*

# MINUTE MOTIVATOR #66

"If you cannot help worrying, remember that worrying cannot help you either. Today is the tomorrow you worried about yesterday. If you worry you die, if you don't worry you die...

*So, why worry?"*

*Now, spend the next one minute meditating and motivating yourself.*

# MINUTE MOTIVATOR #67

# "Change is the essence of life. Be willing to surrender what you are for what you could become."

*Now, spend the next one minute meditating and motivating yourself.*

## MINUTE MOTIVATOR #68

# "Failing to plan means planning to fail. What are your goals?"

*Now, spend the next one minute meditating and motivating yourself.*

# MINUTE MOTIVATOR #69

# "A hug is a great gift - one size fits all, and it's easy to exchange."

*Now, spend the next one minute meditating and motivating yourself.*

# MINUTE MOTIVATOR #70

# "The mark of a successful man is one that has spent an entire day on the bank of a river without feeling guilty about it."

*Now, spend the next one minute meditating and motivating yourself.*

# MINUTE MOTIVATOR #71

# "A genius is a person who shoots at something no one else can see—and hits it."

*Now, spend the next one minute meditating and motivating yourself.*

# MINUTE MOTIVATOR #72

"Defeat may test you; it need not stop you. If at first you don't succeed, try another way. For every obstacle there is a solution. Nothing in the world can take the place of persistence. The greatest mistake is giving up."

*Now, spend the next one minute meditating and motivating yourself.*

# MINUTE MOTIVATOR #73

# "Love is when you take away the feeling, the passion, the romance… and you find out you still care for that person."

*Now, spend the next one minute meditating and motivating yourself.*

# MINUTE MOTIVATOR #74

"There's a difference between interest and commitment. When you're interested in doing something, you do it only when circumstances permit. When you're committed to something, you accept no excuses, only results."

*Now, spend the next one minute meditating and motivating yourself.*

# MINUTE MOTIVATOR #75

# "Beauty is only skin-deep, but ugly goes clear to the bone."

*Now, spend the next one minute meditating and motivating yourself.*

## MINUTE MOTIVATOR #76

# "Many an opportunity is lost because a man is out looking for four-leaf clovers."

*Now, spend the next one minute meditating and motivating yourself.*

# MINUTE MOTIVATOR #77

# "Take twice as long to eat half as much."

*Now, spend the next one minute meditating and motivating yourself.*

## MINUTE MOTIVATOR #78

# "If you cannot help worrying, remember that worrying cannot help you."

*Now, spend the next one minute meditating and motivating yourself.*

# MINUTE MOTIVATOR #79

# "Perpetual worry will get you to one place ahead of time, the cemetery."

*Now, spend the next one minute meditating and motivating yourself.*

# MINUTE MOTIVATOR #80

"Be careful of the words you say, keep them soft and sweet; You never know from day to day which ones you'll have to eat."

*Now, spend the next one minute meditating and motivating yourself.*

## MINUTE MOTIVATOR #81

# "Don't worry if you are a kleptomaniac...

# You can always take something for it."

*Now, spend the next one minute meditating and motivating yourself.*

# MINUTE MOTIVATOR #82

# "The whole world steps aside for the man who knows where he is going."

*Now, spend the next one minute meditating and motivating yourself.*

# MINUTE MOTIVATOR #83

# "To reach a great height a person needs to have great depth."

*Now, spend the next one minute meditating and motivating yourself.*

# MINUTE MOTIVATOR #84

# "Bad habits are like a comfortable bed; they are easy to get into, but hard to get out of."

*Now, spend the next one minute meditating and motivating yourself.*

# MINUTE MOTIVATOR #85

# "A half-baked idea is okay as long as it's in the oven."

*Now, spend the next one minute meditating and motivating yourself.*

# MINUTE MOTIVATOR #86

"Life can either be accepted or changed. If it is not accepted, it must be changed. If it cannot be changed, then it must be accepted."

*Now, spend the next one minute meditating and motivating yourself.*

# MINUTE MOTIVATOR #87

# "Genius is nothing more than inflamed enthusiasm."

*Now, spend the next one minute meditating and motivating yourself.*

# MINUTE MOTIVATOR #88

# "Time wastes our bodies and our wits; but we waste time, so we are quitting."

*Now, spend the next one minute meditating and motivating yourself.*

## MINUTE MOTIVATOR #89

# "Forgiveness is all about me giving up my right to hurt you for hurting me."

*Now, spend the next one minute meditating and motivating yourself.*

# MINUTE MOTIVATOR #90

# "There are no speed limits on the road to excellence."

*Now, spend the next one minute meditating and motivating yourself.*

## MINUTE MOTIVATOR #91

# "You have to do what others won't - to achieve what others don't."

*Now, spend the next one minute meditating and motivating yourself.*

## MINUTE MOTIVATOR #92

# "Any man who knows all the answers most likely misunderstood the questions."

*Now, spend the next one minute meditating and motivating yourself.*

## MINUTE MOTIVATOR #93

# "Achieving starts with believing in yourself."

# Believe in Yourself.

*Now, spend the next one minute meditating and motivating yourself.*

# MINUTE MOTIVATOR #94

# "Tears are words the heart can't express."

*Now, spend the next one minute meditating and motivating yourself.*

# MINUTE MOTIVATOR #95

## "It is easier to believe a lie that you have heard a thousand times, than the truth that you have only heard once."

*Now, spend the next one minute meditating and motivating yourself.*

## MINUTE MOTIVATOR #96

# "The best teachers teach from the heart...

# not from the book."

*Now, spend the next one minute meditating and motivating yourself.*

# MINUTE MOTIVATOR #97

## "It will do no good to argue if you're in the wrong.

## If you're right, you don't need to."

*Now, spend the next one minute meditating and motivating yourself.*

# MINUTE MOTIVATOR #98

# "Winners make goals.

# Losers make excuses!"

*Now, spend the next one minute meditating and motivating yourself.*

# MINUTE MOTIVATOR #99

"There are only two things to worry about:
either you are healthy or you are sick.
If you are healthy, then there is nothing to
worry about. But if you are sick, there are only
two things to worry about: either you will get
well or you will die. If you get well, then there is
nothing to worry about. But, if you die there are
only two things to worry about,
either you will go to heaven or to hell.

If you go to heaven,
then there is nothing to worry about.

*And if you to go hell, you'll be so darn busy
shaking hands with your friends
you won't have time to worry."*

*Now, spend the next one minute meditating and motivating yourself.*

# MINUTE MOTIVATOR #100

"Watch your thoughts; they become words.
Watch your words; they become actions. Watch
your actions; they become habits. Watch your
habits; they become character. Watch your
character; it becomes your destiny."

*Now, spend the next one minute meditating and motivating yourself.*

# CHAPTER 4

# *T*he 7 C's of Success

Now is your time to navigate your vessel along the waters of life found in these seven "C's of Success" If you want to be a total success, you must master these "seven C's" Let's spend one minute a day sailing the "Seven C's".

As you sailed through this book, hopefully you spent one minute a day studying and implementing my One-Minute Motivators. Life can bring some rough seas. If you're not happy with your direction it takes only one minute a day to adjust your sails. From here on we will navigate some new "C's"; these "C's" will now take you to the promised land of SUCCESS. If you can master the Seven "C's", you will cruise to success!

# C - 1: Caring

The vitamin of friendship is B1. If you want a friend, you must be one. This was one of my favorites "One-Minute Motivators". True success in this world is not just based on economic holdings, but personal relationships. We must have a bigger vision than simply accomplishing a goal for personal gain. I believe that people that find true success must have a deep caring for other people. They may have a Type-A personality, or even have an aggressive personality, but you cannot be so tough, or so aggressive, that you run roughshod over others.

Treat everyone with politeness, even those who are rude to you; not because they are nice, but because you are! Becoming a success is more than increasing the digits in your bank account. In life you can always make more money, but time is limited, what you do with your time will determine your character.

# C - 2: Character

Development takes work and discipline. The key is letting each and every experience shape and mold us as we experience them. We must discipline ourselves to always be moving towards our goals and never allowing negative circumstances to destroy us, but instead make us stronger. This is what true success is about!

**The World NEEDS Men and Women...**

- Who cannot be bought
- Whose word is their bond
- Who put character above wealth
- Who possess opinions and a strong will
- Who are larger than their vocations
- Who do not hesitate to take risks
- Who will not lose their individuality in a crowd
- Who will be as honest in small affairs as in greater
- Who will make no compromise with wrong
- Whose ambitions are not confined to their own selfish desires
- Who will not say they do it "Because everybody else does it!"
- Who are true to their friends through good and bad, in adversity as well as in prosperity
- Who do not believe that shrewdness, cunning, and hardheadedness are the best qualities for winning success
- Who are not ashamed or afraid to stand for the truth when it is unpopular
- Who can say "no" with emphasis, although all the rest of the world says "Yes."

# C - 3: Choice

Life is about choices. Each day, from the time we wake up, we make choices. In life every movement you make toward your ultimate success and destiny will be because you choose to move toward it. The actions that you choose each and every day will add up, over the long-term, to your final destination. The power we have as humans to choose is one of the greatest gifts known to mankind. Every art and every inquiry, and similarly every action and choice, is thought to aim at some good; and for this reason, the good has rightly been declared to be that at which all things aim.

# C - 4: Clarity

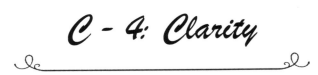

Eighty-percent of success comes from having clarity on who you are, what you believe in, and what you want. People with clarity keep their eyes transfixed on the goal.

Vincent Van Gogh said, *"I experience a period of frightening clarity in those moments when nature is so beautiful. I am no longer sure of myself, and the paintings appear as in a dream."*

# C - 5: Confidence

Success comes to those who have the confidence to try, and the ability and dedication to keep trying till they win. Confidence is something that you cultivate, through affirmations and successful goal setting and attainment. Every success that you achieve, regardless of the magnitude, will grow in your mind and heart. Each passing victory that you achieve builds more and more confidence in yourself. The next time you go to battle on your journey to success, this confidence will give you the power to draw from. Spend **one minute** a day to build confidence inside of yourself so you will be able to dip deeply into that well when you need it!

Michael Jordan said, *"You have to expect things of yourself before you can do them."*

# C - 6: Consistency

People who are successful understand that success does not follow the path of least resistance. Successful people follow a formula. I have found that the "Three P's" (Passion, Purpose, and Perseverance) are my dependable formula for success.

Rocky Balboa had passion and purpose, and he never gave up. Sticking to doing the right things all the time will create your destiny. They consistently do the things that will bring them their success. Consistency is the foundation of success.

# C - 7 Courage

Courage is the one quality we need to succeed, and it is often one of the qualities most in demand and least in supply. Courage is the willingness to do the things you know are right, regardless of the consequences. Leaders are brave people. They know that even success has its challenges, yet they face them head on and move forward consistently, with clarity and confidence toward their goals. Courage is being afraid, but moving forward despite the adversities in front of you.

The key is once you set sail on the "Seven C's" you must stay true to your course. No matter how rocky the "C's" may get, you must never give up. On the following page is a poem (author unknown) to hang on your cabin door, read it daily as you cruise the "Seven C's".

# CHAPTER 5

For many of us often staying motivated can be a daily struggle so I've put together some Simple "**1 Minute**" motivation-boosting tips and words of wisdom for you to take a minute to ponder.

## Fear of failure.

In an article that he wrote for Bloomberg , Mark Cuban stated that he uses the fear of failure for self-motivation.

"No matter what business you're in, you're always at risk -- particularly in technology, where it changes so rapidly you've got to put in the effort to keep up," writes the *Shark Tank* panel member. "There's always the opportunity for some 18-year-old to come out of nowhere and crush you-that motivates the hell out of me."

## Surround yourself with highly successful and motivated people.

"No one does it alone," said Mark Zuckerberg during a Q & A in 2016. "When you look at most big things that get done in the world, they're not done by one person, so you're going to need to build a team."

When building your All-Star team, seek out people who excel in the areas where you're not strong or have less experience. "You're going to need people that have complementary skills," Zuckerberg emphasized. "No matter how talented you are, there are just going to be things that you don't bring to the table."

## Never feel sorry yourself.

"All of my best successes came on the heels of a failure, so I've learned to look at each belly flop as the beginning of something good," said Barbara Corcoran, founder of The Corcoran Group and Shark on *Shark Tank*.

"If you just hang in there, you'll find that something is right around the corner. It's that belief that keeps me motivated. I've learned not to feel sorry for myself, ever. Just five minutes of feeling sorry for yourself takes your power away and makes you unable to see the next opportunity."

## Keep affirmations where you can see them.

"It's so easy as an entrepreneur to get sucked into feeling exhausted or frustrated, and often the blame is yours alone," writes Murray Newlands, founder of online invoicing company Sighted. "But a negative mindset sucks up mental bandwidth and energy that you need to stay focused and successful.

"It is crucial to maintain an optimistic attitude in the face of setbacks. Whenever you see a quote or a picture that helps you stay positive, place it front and center so you can remember what this journey is all about."

## Leverage the power of rejection.

"On June 26, 2008, our friend Michael Seibel introduced us to seven prominent investors in Silicon Valley. We were attempting to raise $150,000 at a $1.5M valuation. That means for $150,000 you could have bought 10 percent of Airbnb."

"Below you will see five rejections. The other two did not reply," writes Airbnb Co-Founder Brian Chesky on Medium.

"The investors that rejected us were smart people, and I am sure we didn't look very impressive at the time."

Today Airbnb is valued at just under $30 billion.

## Do what you're passionate for.

This is the key. However, as Chalmers Brown, co-founder and CTO of Due writes, "We want to not only make a lot of money but enjoy what we do as well. We are willing to take on the risk of unstable pay in exchange for following our dreams."

"Unfortunately, your dream job may not always be the best decision financially. Sometimes your hobbies are best kept as projects in your spare time for fun (which is great!). If you do want to try to turn your passion into a full-time job, these tips can help you get started the right way."

Brown gives the tips below:

- Improve something that you're already doing.
- Figuring out where market.
- Sharing your passion with others.
- Stay happy and motivated by assigning tasks that you're not a fan of to someone else.

## When The Going Gets Tough

When things get tough, it's time to take"1Minute" to regroup,re-motivate and turn things around. I like many people turn to a motivational quotes for a bit of inspiration. Some of these powerful sayings have become celebrated parts of society's lexicon. Some of my favorites include:

*"I have not failed. I've just found 10,000 ways that won't work."*
*-Thomas Edison*

*"No one can make you feel inferior without your consent."*
*-Eleanor Roosevelt*

*"If you can't fly then run, if you can't run then walk, if you can't walk then crawl, but whatever you do you have to keep moving forward."*
*-Rev. Martin Luther King, Jr.*

But out of all of the things that people-famous, influential, and otherwise-have to say, what makes some turns of phrase so powerful that they become mantras for generations?

Depending on whom you ask, the appeal appears to lie in a combination of good wordsmithing, motivational psychology, and a measure of self-selection. Obviously, people like myself who tend to feel inspired by motivational quotes are going to find them more resonant than those who don't find simple phrases and sayings to be particularly meaningful. It only takes **"1 Minute"** to appreciate and digest a good quote or saying.

## THE COACHING FACTOR

As a coach I believe there's an innate self-selection process that narrows the population of people who get Inspired by motivational sayings. If you or a teacher, coach, or mentor believes you can do something, you're more likely to do it. it takes **"1 Minute"** per idea to affirm you like yourself, believe in yourself.

With affirmations there's there is a little bit of implicit coaching that's happening when you're reading it. It's building that self-efficacy in that kind of dialogue that you're having with yourself, this **"1 Minute** Motivators" make a difference

# THE POWER OF LANGUAGE

There's also power in the words themselves, people have an "appetite for well-expressed wisdom, motivational or otherwise."

Students of Latin see examples of aphorisms from 2,000 years ago, such as *ubi concordia, ibi victoria,* 'where there is unity, there is victory.' Usually, these sayings involve some keen insight put into memorable wording. They are little triumphs of rhetoric, in the old and positive sense of the word.

Words from recognized leaders in business, politics, and the arts may also hold more gravitas because of the assumption that when people are in public positions, they must be accomplished, wise, or otherwise exceptional to have achieved those positions. Those perceptions can make messages from such leaders more powerful.

When people open to a strong message, well-structured messages that use strong imagery and appeal to our aspirational nature, it can be meaningful and powerful in changing our thinking and helping us see something in ourselves that we want to change or overcome. Let me share with you some "**1 Minute**s" words of Wisdom.

# 1-Minute Words of Wisdom

- Don't compare your life to others. You have no idea what their journey is all about.
- Don't have negative thoughts or things you cannot control. Instead, invest your energy in the positive present moment.
- Don't over-do, know your limits.
- Don't take yourself so seriously.
- No one else does.
- Don't waste your precious energy on gossip.
- Dream more while you are awake.
- Envy is a waste of time.
- You already have all you need.
- Forget issues of the past.
- Don't remind your partner of his or her mistakes of the past; that will ruin your present happiness.
- Life is too short to waste time hating anyone.
- Don't hate others.
- Make peace with your past so it won't spoil the present.

- No one is in charge of your happiness except you.
- Realize that life is a school and you are here to learn.
- Problems are simply part of the curriculum that appear and fade away like algebra class, but the lessons you learn will last a lifetime.
- Smile and laugh more. You don't have to win every argument.
- Agree to disagree.
- Call your family often.
- Each day give something good to others.
- Forgive everyone for everything.
- Spend time with people over the age of 70 and under the age of 6.
- Try to make at least 3 people smile each day.
- What other people think of you is none of your business.
- Your job won't take care of you when you are sick.
- Your friends will. Stay in touch. Do the right thing!
- Get rid of anything that isn't useful, beautiful, or joyful.
- God heals everything.
- However good or bad a situation is, it will change.
- No matter how you feel, get up, dress up, and show up.
- The best is yet to come.
- When you awake alive in the morning, thank God for it.

# CHAPTER 6

Let's face the facts, we are all products of nature. Take " **1 Minute**" to think of yourself as no different than a caterpillar-now picture yourself breaking forth and fly as a butterfly. Once you believe, you can achieve. Once you have faith, you are free to follow your dreams and find your destiny. To some, The Secret is a best-selling book; to others it's nothing more than an understanding of belief. "I AM" is a belief system that each of us can tap into. Personal greatness and achievements afford us the power to overcome any obstacle, but obstacles are what make life an adventure. By using your super-conscious mind, the world is your oyster.

Many of the world's greatest thinkers have identified this inner power and presented a name for it. Ralph Waldo Emerson called it oversoul. He said, "We lie in the lap of an immense intelligence that responds to our every need." Napoleon Hill referred to this power as "an infinite intelligence." He claimed that the ability to access this intelligence was the key to the wealthy men and women he had researched over the years. D. D. Palmer and B. J. Palmer, the founders of chiropractic, recognized this power as innate intelligence, a universal intelligence. We must now tap into the power that lies within us to achieve what we want, what we need, what we are entitled to. The super-conscious mind is our infinite source of creativity. All truly classical art, music, and literature comes from people who have tapped into this creative power. We start to use our super-conscious mind when we dream and set goals, when we turn the invisible into the visible. Although through our education we have come to acknowledge a traditional direct approach, many of us have yet to fully believe or understand the infinite reservoir of power we harbor or how to fully utilize this power. Why something so simple appears so complex is baffling. Yet the Emersons, Edisons, Mozarts, Bachs, Beethovens, and Disneys all came to master this principle and we can, too. By mastering time, by mastering your One Minutes, you can master your life and rule your destiny.

Dennis Whatley said, "Failure is only a temporary change in direction to set you straight for your next success."

**Through the course of life, I have formulated five basic principles:**

1. Life is difficult. It always has been and always will be.

2. Everything "I am" to be is up to me.

3. You can learn anything you need to learn, become anyone you want to become, achieve anything you want to achieve.

4. Life has few limitations, and most of those are on the inside, not the outside.

5. The sky is not the limit; the sky is only as far as we can see. The universe is infinite, and so we have no limits.

Now let me share with you some 1-Minute Things to Remember every day.

# *1-Minute Things to Remember*

- Your presence is a present to the world.
- You're unique and one of a kind.
- Your life can be what you want it to be.
- Take the days just one at a time.
- Count your blessings, not your troubles.
- You'll make it through whatever comes along.
- Within you are so many answers.
- Understand, have courage, be strong.
- Don't put limits on yourself. So many dreams are waiting to be realized.
- Decisions are too important to leave to chance.
- Reach for your peak, your goal, your prize.
- Nothing wastes more energy than worrying.
- The longer one carries a problem, the heavier it gets.
- Don't take things too seriously.
- Live a life of serenity, not a life of regrets.
- Remember that a little love goes a long way...
  Remember that a lot... goes forever.
- Remember that friendship is a wise investment.
- Life's treasures are people... together.
- Realize that it's never too late.
- Do ordinary things in an extraordinary way.
- Have health and hope and happiness.
- Take time to wish upon a star.

# *"Don't Quit"*

*When things go wrong, as they sometimes will,*
*When the road you're trudging seems all uphill,*
*When the funds are low and the debts are high,*
*And you want to smile but you have to sigh,*
*When care is pressing you down a bit—*
*Rest if you must, but don't you quit.*
*Life is odd with its twists and turns,*
*As everyone sometimes learns.*
*And many a person turns about*
*When an individual might have won had he or she stuck it out.*
*Don't give up though the pace seems slow—*
*You may succeed with yet another blow.*
*Often the goal is nearer than it seems*
*To a faint and faltering woman or man;*
*Often the struggler has given up*
*When he or she might have captured the victor's cup;*
*And one learned too late when the night came down,*
*How close he or she was to the golden crown.*
*Success is failure turned inside out—*
*The silver tint of the clouds of doubt,*
*And when you never can tell how close you are,*
*It may be near when it seems afar;*
*So stick to the fight when you're hardest hit—*
*It's when things seem worst, you mustn't quit.*

And don't ever forget… for even a day… How very special you are. It only takes "**1 Minute**" a day to plant the seeds of success, the seeds of greatness. And if we are to succeed by planting these seeds, then we must weed out the negatives in our life. If we allow these weeds to grow, they will strangle all that is good within us and then we will be without. We must plan our "**1 Minute**" daily, setting our goals, stating our affirmations, and moving into our zone.

# CHAPTER 7
## *Dr. Kaplan's Top Ten Youthful Aging Tips*

One of the keys to being Motivated, is staying healthy. As we come to near the end of my book let me share some **1 Minute** Health Motivators.

Youthful aging doesn't have to mean turning to cosmetic surgery or chemicals. If you really want to look younger and stay healthy, here are my top ten tips for youthful aging:

### 1. Quit Smoking

One of the most important youthful aging tips of all. If I could do it, you can. It only takes "**1 Minute**" to make up your mind to quit, that minute may save your life.

Friends, if you smoke, STOP NOW. It's as simple as that. Over time, you may able to completely reverse the damage smoking has done to your skin and you'll for sure stop the damage from getting worse. With the right youthful aging  skin care, proper nutrition, and a good multi-vitamin—you should begin to look younger and healthier than you have for years, if we could do it so could you.

Smokers do not usually have healthy skin. So, do your face, your body, your lungs a favor and quit smoking now. Kick start your cessation program with acupuncture or laser therapy. You're more likely to succeed with help than by trying to quit cold turkey.

If you do choose to continue smoking be prepared for the conse- quences. Smoking accelerates skin aging by en- couraging the destruction of collagen. Reduced levels of collagen are one of the primary reasons your skin ages, so a smoker's skin ages much faster. The tell-tale signs are dull, grayish, dry skin, increased wrinkling around the eyes, and  the puckering wrinkles from drawing on cigarettes, known as "smoker's face." *Is it really what you want for your skin?*

## 2. Protect Your Skin From the Sun

Sun damage is the number one enemy of younger looking skin. My friend Dr. Harold Rosen, a plastic surgeon who treated me for skin cancer still yells at me on the golf course, "Wear a hat; use sunscreen."

Where did my wrinkles come from? How did I get into this mess? The sun, naturally. As a youth, I overdid it on my days at the Belmar, New Jersey beach.

Getting a suntan leads to photo-aging, a process that produces deep wrinkles in leathery textured skin and will cause premature age spots. Use a moisturizer combined with a broad-spectrum sunscreen. Always have sunscreen with you. If you want a tan— fake, it—most of Hollywood does. *Putting on sunscreen, only takes "1 Minute"!*

## 3. Eat A Natural and High Antioxidant Rich Diet

Antioxidants are a group of vitamins, minerals, and carotenoids that work against the damage caused by free radicals that weaken the skin's structure. For maximum youthful aging protection eat fresh fruit, vegetables, fruit, and whole grains. For younger looking skin and a healthier immune system make sure you get plenty of vitamins A, C, E, and Sele*nium; I call these my 4 ACES. These vitamins work together to restore collagen in your cells. You also need plenty of omega-3 essential fatty acids, which will aid in a healthy heart. Omega-3s maintain the structure and fluidity of cells and help moisturize the skin from within—an essential part of your youthful aging diet. Taking Omega 3's only takes "*1 Minute*"*!*

## 4. Take A Vitamin Supplement For Younger Looking Skin

Boost your antioxidant intake with a daily supplement. Go for one with the highest levels of the key vitamins and minerals for younger looking skin and all-round health. *Taking daily vitamins only takes "*1 Minute*"!*

## 5. Add Green Tea To Your Day

Drinking green tea is a youthful aging tip you may not have considered. Green tea is an amazing youthful aging powerhouse. Recent research findings show that taking sufficient green tea during the day can protect you from all forms of cancer, build your resistance to heart disease and dementia, and contribute to your body's ability to burn fat, especially abdominal fat, resulting in possible weight loss and increased energy, even when there is no change in your daily diet. To get the wonderful youthful aging effects of green tea in concentrated form, take a high strength green tea powder. *Have a cup of tea, it only takes "*1 Minute*"!*

## 6. Moisturize And Exfoliate

A great youthful aging moisturizer, when applied properly, will provide continuous hydration—essential for mature skin—and protection from further free-radical damage. Choose the best moisturizer you can afford. Make sure it has high levels of proven effective ingredients like peptides that work to reverse the aging process and reduce wrinkles.

You have to exfoliate for younger looking skin. Without exfoliation youthful aging skin creams can't work their magic on the skin. Follow a disciplined and consistent skin routine and exfoliate at least twice a week to ensure that fresh, live skin is soaking up moisture. My wife Bonnie is great at this, and I am so proud of her. *Exfoliate, it only takes* "**1 Minute**"*!*

## 7. Exercise more

Exercise is part of my life. I don't love doing it, I love the way I feel after. Exercise is my key youthful aging tip. It will give you more energy, build muscle mass, increase blood flow to your skin, help prevent high blood pressure, reduce anxiety, strengthen bones, and raise your metabolic rate so you lose more weight more quickly.

With all these youthful aging benefits—exercise doesn't have to be a chore. Go for exercise that gives you a cardio workout as well as developing core strength and fighting abdominal, buttocks, and thigh fat. So, if you haven't already, put exercise at the heart of your youthful aging routine. *It takes more than* "**1 Minute**"*, but it only takes only takes* "**1 Minute**" *to start!*

## 8. Moderate Your Alcohol Intake

 My wife and I still enjoy a glass of wine. Wine is loaded with phenolic compounds and flavonoids, with a high antioxidant value. The key is doing it in moderation. We all know that drinking too much can lead to serious health problems. What is less talked about is the aging effect of alcohol on the skin. Alcohol is bad for your skin, as it has an inflammatory and dehydrating action that accelerates the aging process. Excess alcohol blocks the absorption of key nutrients you need for antioxidant protection. The key is drink eight ounces of water for every four ounces of wine and two ounces of regular alcohol. *Drinking an extra glass of water only takes* "**1 Minute**"*!*

## 9. Stress Less

We are all under pressure in life. Pressure to perform, to be the best dad, best mom, best employee. We all feel the pressure to succeed. Athletes feel pressure to win. Pressure is part of life, just accept it and don't let it into your consciousness. Once you do, once you obsess over pressure, then pressure becomes stress. When you're under stress your body releases stress hormones that, over a period of time, suppress the immune system and accelerate the aging process. As a result of prolonged stress, the cells in your body— including your skin cells—are unable to regenerate properly and become more susceptible to the aging process. The result is premature lines and wrinkles. Stress really does get etched on your face. So youthful aging tip number nine is to learn to recognize that pressure is okay, but stress is not, so manage it effectively. Meditate, each day, only takes "**1 Minute**" to start!

## 10. Drink More Water

Nothing on this planet would survive without water. Not cola—water. You need to hydrate your body, your skin, from within. Skin cells need water just like every part of your body including your brain. Without sufficient water your skin will dehydrate, and essential youthful aging nutrients cannot be delivered to your system. You should aim to drink around eight 8-ounce glasses every day just to replace the water you lose through sweating and urination. To look good, and for a longer time, you need to make sure water is an essential part of your youthful aging routine.

Just about every dermatologist out there tells us we should drink water for skin health and to hydrate the skin. I did a quick review and found that respected dermatologists like Daniel Maes (Head of Research for Estée Lauder), Nicholas Perricone, Dr. Murad, and countless others less famous but no less qualified all say drinking water is important to keep skin hydrated. And hydrated skin is younger looking skin as we all know.

Loss of hydration in the skin shows in all sorts of ways—dryness, tightness, flakiness. Dry skin has less resilience and is more prone to wrinkling. Water is essential to maintain skin moisture and is the vehicle for delivering essential nutrients to the skin cells. As water is lost in large quantities every day—it stands to reason you have to replace it somehow. Drink enough water during the day to maintain the skin's moisture level. *The key is to drink water throughout the day at regular intervals, this makes it easy and fun.*

That's it—10 great youthful aging tips to help you look younger and feel great—all you need to do is spend "**1 Minute**" or more per day and follow them!

Imagine a life where you could be healthier and happier. This is why my book is so important. In my book, The 5 minute Motivator I share with the reader my quest for health happiness and success. **www.5minutemotivator.com**

If you're like means want so start quest for health, happiness, success, you may ask, "Where do I begin?" We begin with the basics. Let's start looking to the earth for our products and let's provide our cells with the antioxidants they need to provide telomere support to prevent aging.

Let's start today to make our lives our bodies a better place to live in. Imagine just "**1 Minute**" a day can change your life forever. This is a small price to pay for a large return—health.

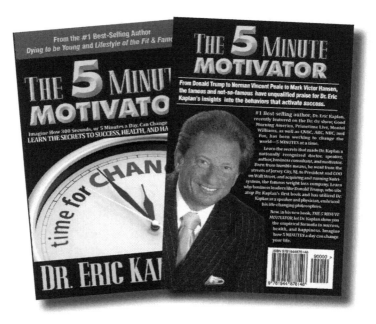

# CHAPTER 8

## *Stories of Motivation From Hollywood & Beyond*

There are no "**1 Minute**" shortcuts to health, happiness or success and if we do not accept this truism, we will find ourselves in the position of the young contractor in a story told by Charles Tremendous Jones:

"It seems this young contractor was married to a contractor's daughter. The father-in-law wanted to give the young man a boost in his career.

*"Son,"* he said, *"I don't want you to start at the bottom where I did. So I want you to go out and build the most tremendous house this town has ever seen, put the best of everything in it, make it a palace, and turn it over to me."*

Well, this was an opportunity to make a killing. He hurried out to slap together a building that would survive two fairly stiff gales. In short order, he was back to dear old dad. *"Well, Dad, it's finished."*

*"Is this the palace like I asked?"*

"Yes-siree, Dad,"

*"Is it really the finest house ever built, Son?"*

"Yes-siree, Dad."

*"All right, where is the bill? Is there a good profit in it for you?"*

"Yes-siree, Dad."

*"Very good. Here is your check, and where is the deed?"*

As he looked at the deed, the father said, *"I didn't tell you why I wanted that house to be the best house ever built. I wanted to do something special for you and my daughter to show you how much I love you... Here, take the deed, go live in the house – you built for yourself."*

---

The young gold-bricker crept out a shattered, frustrated man. He thought he was making a fortune at his father-in-law's expense by saving money on inferior material and short-cuts, **he cheated only himself.**

Success takes commitment and I'm asking you to commit "**1 Minute**" each hour, each day to empowering yourself. The power of commitment is behind every success story, including the following:

### Gail Borden-Borden's Milk & Ice Cream
An eccentric inventor and drifter, witnesses the deaths of a number of children who drank contaminated milk. He finds a way to preserve milk so that such tragedies will not recur.

### George Kinney-Kinney Shoes
A widower with a young son loses his job at a department store. He dreams of becoming his own boss and scrapes together $1,500 to open his own shoe store.

### Thomas Alva Edison - (Inventor of the light bulb, phonograph, motion picture, and much more!)
A six-year-old boy ponders ways to speed up the hatching of chicken eggs. His solution is to sit on the eggs himself. This initial glimmer of ingenuity was the precursor to the genius that later illuminated (literally) the world.

### Estee Lauder-Estee Lauder Cosmetics and Skin Care Products
The little girl enjoys touching people's faces and hair, she loves to help make people more attractive. She dreams of becoming a skin care specialist while she watches her uncle concoct creams and potions on her mother's gas stove.

### Mike Ditka-Pro football player; head coach
Living in a government-funded housing project in Pennsylvania, he dreams of escaping the mines of his home state. He knows sports but more important, he knows what he wants.

### Burton Baskin and Irvine Robbins of Baskin-Robbins Ice Cream

Two brothers-in-law have a simple dream of starting a business together and earning $75 a week. Their marketing philosophy is simple, simply brilliant: they will serve one product 31 different ways.

### Robert, Edward, and James Johnson
### Johnson & Johnson Health Care Products

It's the 19th century, and may surgery patients are dying from infections caused by unsanitary conditions. A young dreamer convinces his brothers to work with him on finding a way to produce sterile bandages.

### Dick Clark-American Bandstand host

After his older brother is shot down and killed in World War II, the teenager listens to the radio to ease his loneliness. He dreams of someday being an announcer on his own show.

### Babe Ruth "The Sultan of SWAT"

The Babe, was successful at hitting 714 lifetime runs. A total that many felt would never be equaled, a feat so spectacular that even today, years after his death, he is still a legend to every child or every person who ever enters the game of baseball. But, he also was the man who struck out a record of 1,732 times. *The point here is, we as people will be remembered more for our successes than our failures.*

As Jiminy Cricket in Pinocchio said, "Accentuate the positive, eliminate the negative." Consider these goal setters who stuck to their goals regardless of any adversity:

- After **Fred Astaire's** first screen test, the memo from the testing director of MGM said, "Can't act. Can't sing. Balding. Can dance a little." Astaire kept that memo over the fireplace of his Beverly Hills home.

- An expert said of **Vince Lombardi,** "He possesses minimal football knowledge, lacks motivation."
- **Socrates** was called an immoral corrupter of youth.
- **Louisa May Alcott,** author of Little Women, was encouraged to find work as a servant or seamstress by her family.
- **Beethoven** handled a violin awkward-ly and preferred creating his own com-positions to improving his technique. His teacher called him a "hopeless composer." He continued to compose even though he went deaf.
- The parents of the famous opera singer **Enrico Caruso** wanted him to become an engineer. His teacher said he had no voice at all.
- **Charles Darwin,** the father of the theory of evolution, gave up a medical career and was told by his father, "You care for nothing but shooting dogs and rat-catching." In his autobiography, Darwin wrote, "I was considered by all my masters, and by my father, a very ordinary boy, rather below the common standard of intellect."
- **Walt Disney** was fired by a newspaper editor for lack of ideas. He also went bankrupt several times.
- **Albert Einstein** did not speak until he was four years old and did not read until he was seven. His teacher described him as mentally slow, unsociable, and adrift forever in his false dreams. He was expelled from one school and refused admit-tance to the Zurich Polytechnic School.
- **Louis Pasteur** was recognized as only a mediocre pupil in un-dergraduate studies and ranked 15th out of 22 in chemistry class.
- **Isaac Newton** did very poorly in grade school.
- The sculptor **Rodin's** father said, "I have an idiot for a son." Described as the worst pupil in school, Rodin failed three times to secure admittance to the school of art. His uncle called him uneducable.
- **Leo Tolstoy,** author of War and Peace, flunked out of college. He was described as unable and unwilling to learn.

- Playwright **Tennessee Williams** was enraged when his play, Me, Vasha, was not chosen in a class competition at Washington University where he was a student in English. The teacher recalls that Williams denounced the judges' choices and their intelligence.
- **F. W. Woolworth's** employees at the dry goods store claimed that he did not have enough sense to wait upon customers.
- **Henry Ford** failed and went broke 5 times before he finally succeeded.
- **Babe Ruth,** considered by many sports historians to be the greatest athlete of all time, is famous for setting the home run record of 714 home runs. He also holds the record for strike-outs: Babe Ruth struck out over 3,000 times.
- **Winston Churchill** failed 6th grade. He did not become Prime Minister of England until he was 62 and only then after a life-time of defeats and setbacks. His greatest contributions came when he was a senior citizen.
- Eighteen publishers turned down **Richard Bach's** 10,000-word story about a soaring seagull, Jonathan Livingston Seagull, before Macmillan finally published it in 1970. By 1975, it had sold more than 7,000,000 copies in the United States alone.
- **Richard Herker** worked 7 years on his humorous war novel, M.A.S.H., only to have it rejected by 21 publishers before Morrow decided to publish it. It became a runaway bestseller, spawning a blockbuster movie and a highly successful television series.

**Abraham Lincoln.**

I think of Lincoln primarily as the president who brought our country through a bitter civil war, the man who ended slavery. I also knew that he did not begin life with the trappings of success. I was stunned to read the following concerning Lincoln:

*1816 Forced from his home*
*1818 His mother died*
*1831 Failed in business*
*1832 Defeated for State Legislature*
*1833 Failed in business again*

*1834 Elected to State Legislature*
*1835 His sweetheart died*
*1836 Suffered a nervous breakdown*
*1838 Defeated for Speaker of State Legislature*
*1840 Defeated for Elector*
*1843 Defeated for Congress*
*1846 Elected to Congress*
*1848 Lost reelection*
*1854 Rejected for job of Land Officer*
*1855 Defeated for Senate*
*1856 Defeated for Vice President*
*1858 Defeated for Senate*
*1860 Elected President of the United States of America*

Here was a person with a dream so strong, no failure could dampen it. We were all taught about his greatness. Now I understand that Lincoln's greatness stemmed from his perseverance. In 28 years of politics, he had four times as many defeats as victories. Most men would have decided that life was unfair and given up. Because Lincoln remained true to his goals, he eventually won the most important race of all. In 1860, not only was he elected as President of the United States, but he went on to become one of the greatest presidents our country has ever known.

None of these people were overnight successes, nor should you become discouraged if you don't instantaneously produce tangible results. It takes more than one minute to achieve all your goals, but remember, each day, each hour, each week, each month, each year, each life all begins with **1 Minute**... the first minute. ***May this book open your eyes to the power of 60 seconds, or one minute!***

# 1-MINUTE MOTIVATOR

## *1-Minute Commandments for Success*

✳ Picture the positives.

✳ Eliminate the negatives.

✳ Focus on your strengths.

✳ Eliminate your limits.

✳ Meditate.

✳ Plan with positive people.

✳ Ride elevators with the elevated.

✳ Remember there is only one you in the universe!

✳ Live your dreams, not someone else's.

✳ Throw "never," "won't," and "can't" out of your vocabulary."

# *Remember...*

The purpose of this book is to empower, inspire and enable people to take a "**1 Minute**" approach to their health and happiness. We can each enhance our health, happiness and well-being one cell, one minute at a time.

 I like to end each of my lectures with saying "The past is history; the future is a mystery, but this moment of life is a gift, and that is why we call it 'The Present'." Take the next "**1 Minute** ", to give thanks to your present and unwrap your gift, the gift of life.

I dedicate every moment of my gift, of my Present, especially this "One Minute" to coordinate conventional and alternative medicine into our system so that a sickness-based model will part of the future. A world with happy, healthy, motivated, inspired people.

## I hope I inspired you.

## *And if I did, now I ask you to inspire others.*

# CHAPTER 9

## *"The True Value of Time"*

### TO REALIZE THE VALUE OF ONE YEAR

Talk to a student who failed a grade and was held back.

### TO REALIZE THE VALUE OF ONE MONTH

Talk to a mother who gave birth to a premature baby.

### TO REALIZE THE VALUE OF ONE WEEK

Talk to the editor of a weekly newspaper.

### TO REALIZE THE VALUE OF ONE HOUR

Talk to the person holding on for his or her life.

### TO REALIZE THE VALUE OF ONE MINUTE

Talk to a person who missed their plane.

### TO REALIZE THE VALUE OF ONE SECOND

Talk to a person who just avoided an accident.

Treasure every second, every minute and every hour, of every day, for the rest of your life. Live each day as it is your last. My wife and I were as close to death as you can come, we appreciate the little things and realize life is for living. At the end of your life you only have three things that matter: your friends, your family, and your memories. During my coma, it was these three things that I held on to, that I cherished, that brought me back to life. If you were told you were going to die, how much would you pay for one more hour with your family? *It is at these moments that we realize that time, not money, is life's most valuable commodity. Live.*

It is at these moments that we realize that time, not money, is life's most valuable commodity. Live a life with no regrets and give thanks to your friends and family because they shared their time and their life with you. **They believed you were someone special enough to spend their lives with you.**

The future is right here, right now. Take the time to write down your goals and create a personal plan of action to get what you want out of life. Invest your 86,400 seconds a day wisely. To change yourself, to change your life, it takes only 60 seconds - only "**1 Minute**:"

**Don't spend another second, minute, hour, day, month, or year of your life settling for less than you deserve.**

Give life all you've got. Life is not only a challenge, but an opportunity. Life is complex with its paradoxes of pain and pleasure, success and failure. You just need to search within yourself. I challenge you to get excited about life. You have 86,400 seconds every day to make a difference. Use them wisely. Spend "**1 Minute**" (minimum) per day unlocking the miracle of motivation, the power of goals, the strength of affirmations and you will awaken The Master Motivator, "The Wizard Within".

### THE CLOCK IS TICKING.

# Go to work!

# 1-Minute Traits of a Good Leader

**Honesty-**Display sincerity, integrity, and candor in all your actions. Deceptive behavior will not inspire trust.

**Competent-**Base your actions on reason and moral principles. Do not make decisions based on childlike emotional desires or feelings.

**Forward-looking-**Set goals and have a vision of the future. The vision must be owned throughout the organization. Effective leaders envision what they want and how to get it. They habitually pick priorities stemming from their basic values.

**Inspiring-**Display confidence in all that you do. By showing endurance in mental, physical, and spiritual stamina, you will inspire others to reach for new heights. Take charge when necessary.

**Intelligent-**Read, study, and seek challenging assignments.

**Fair-minded-**Show fair treatment to all people. Prejudice is the enemy of justice. Display empathy by being sensitive to the feelings, values, interests, and well-being of others.

**Broad-minded-**Seek out diversity.

**Courageous-**Have the perseverance to accomplish a goal, regardless of the seemingly insurmountable obstacles. Display a confident calmness when under stress.

**Straightforward-**Use sound judgment to make good decisions at the right time.

**Imaginative-**Make timely and appropriate changes in your thinking, plans, and methods. Show creativity by thinking of new and better goals, ideas, and solutions to problems. Be innovative!

Successful people think successful thoughts. The genocide to success is bad thinking. Imagine legendary Dallas Cowboys coach Tom Landry who, during his first season with the Cowboys, didn't win a single game. His record was zero wins, eleven losses, and one tie. Yet he went on to become one of the most successful coaches in their franchise history. He never gave in to the media or the ridicule; he knew he was a winner and kept telling himself that, as well.

I encourage you to turn your personality into a success personality. Understand that the only psychology to success is the desire to succeed. You may be wondering what your personality has to do with your health. Many studies suggest that we can think our way to health-or illness. One such study conducted by John W. Shaffer and Pirkko L. Graves at Johns Hopkins University School of Medicine revealed that men who hide their feelings are much more likely to develop cancer than men who express their feelings. The researchers also found that loners were 16 times more likely to get cancer than emotionally expressive men.

It only takes **"1 Minute"** a day to recite daily affirmations.

Through affirmations, we can express our feelings, needs, and desires with confidence that they can be fulfilled.

"I am now at my optimum weight."
"I enjoy excellent health and limitless vitality."

"All of my relationships are loving and fulfilling."
"I love my work and always do an excellent job."

## Let's look at Dr Seuss's affirmation in regards to work:

*I love my job,*
*I love the pay*
*I love it more and more each day*
*I love my boss, he is the best*
*I love his boss and all the rest*
*I love my office and its location*
*I hate to have to go on vacation*
*I love my furniture, drab and grey, and piles of paper that grow each day!*
*I think my job is really swell, there's nothing else I love so well.*
*I love to work among my peers,*
*I love their leers, and jeers, and sneers.*
*I love my computer and its software;*
*I hug it often though it won't care.*
*I love each program and every file.*
*I'd love them more if they worked a while.*
*I am happy to be here.*
*I am.*
*I am.*
*I'm the happiest slave of the Firm, I am.*
*I love this work,*
*I love these chores.*
*I love the meetings with deadly bores.*
*I love my job; I'll say it again,*
*I even love those friendly men.*
*Those friendly men who've come today.*
*In clean white coats to take me away!!!*

Feel free to make your own affirmations using the language that feels right for your particular situation and goals. You hold in your heart the key to the treasure of affirmations.

One of the main keys is just being happy with yourself. Stop worrying about what you don't have and start appreciating what you do have. Affirm your uniqueness regardless of your job, position, or station in life. It's your attitude, your love of life that is your greatest asset. Let me share a story with you.

One day an American investment banker was at the pier of a small coastal Mexican village when a small boat with just one fisherman docked one afternoon. Inside the small boat were several large yellowfin tuna. The American complimented the Mexican on the quality of his fish and asked how long it took to catch them.

The Mexican replied, "Only a little while."

The American then asked, "Why didn't you stay out longer and catch more fish?"

The Mexican said, "Why, with this I have more than enough to support my family's needs."

The American then asked, "But what do you do during a normal day?"

The Mexican fisherman said, "I sleep late till about 10, have a little coffee with my wife, play with my children, then I go fish a little. Then I come home, clean my fish, and take siesta with my wife, Maria. When I awake, we stroll into the village each evening where I sip wine and play guitar with my amigos. I have a full and busy life."

The American scoffed, "I'm a Yale MBA and I'm positive I could change your life. You should spend more time fishing and with the proceeds buy a bigger boat: With the proceeds from the bigger boat you could buy several boats. Eventually you would have a fleet of fishing boats. Instead of selling your catch to a middleman you would sell directly to the processor; eventually opening your own cannery. You would control the product, processing and distribution. You will eventually need to leave this small coastal fishing village and move to Mexico City, then Florida and eventually New York where you will run your ever-expanding enterprise."

The Mexican fisherman asked, "But, how long will this all take?"

To which the American replied, "15 to 20 years." "But what then?" asked the Mexican.

The American smiled, laughed and said that's the best part. "When the time is right you would announce an IPO and sell your company stock to the public and become very rich, you would make millions." "Millions?... Then what?"

The American said, "Then you would retire. Move to a small coastal fishing village where you would sleep late, fish a little, play with your kids, take siesta with your wife, stroll to the village in the evenings where you could sip wine and play your guitar with your amigos."

The Mexican smiled, shook his head and walked away.

Each and every one of us has so much, yet we always want so much more, forgetting that what we already have may be perfect. Take "**1 Minute**" every day to appreciate you, your life and affirm your future. The knowledge of who we are, and what we will act as, is an antidote for any epidemic.

It's simple to say that we must always start at the beginning. Each day has a beginning and an end, as does each project, goal, story, attitude, etc. The beauty of new days is that they offer new beginnings. William James said, "Believe that life is worth living and your belief will create the fact." Let us forget yesterday, concentrate on today, and prepare for tomorrow.

It only takes "**1 Minute**" each day to plant the seeds of success, the seeds of greatness. And if we are to succeed by planting these seeds, then we must weed out the negatives in our life. If we allow these weeds to grow, they will strangle all that is good within us and then we will be without. We must plan our "**1 Minute**" daily, setting our goals, stating our affirmations, and moving into our zone.

As the sun rises and the sun sets, our life is controlled and coordinated by time. Our day consists of 86,400 seconds. How to utilize this time is our choice. It truly demonstrates the age-old creed that all men are created equal. All men and all women share the same amount of time. They have the same opportunity in every given day; it's a matter of how they utilize their time. By utilizing and implementing time, we can increase production, which will produce higher levels of fulfillment and self-esteem

# CHAPTER 10
# $\mathcal{F}$inal Thoughts

Now is your time, your minute, your hour, your day, your week, your month, your year to fulfill your dreams. It only takes one minute here and there to master your destiny. To access your treasures, you must utilize these keys. Spend a minimum of one minute each day over the next 21 days mastering each and every one of the keys and watch it unlock your future success.

Remember that time, not money, is life's most valuable commodity. Live a life with no regrets and give thanks to your friends and family because they shared their time and their life with you. They believed you were someone special enough to spend their lives with you. Remember that time waits for no one.

Take our final "minutes" to remember:
**The past is history.**
**The future is a mystery.**
**But this moment of life, right here, right now is the gift.**
**That is why we call it the PRESENT.**
I challenge you now to appreciate your gift and make use of your present. The future is right here, right now. Take the time to write down your goals and create a personal plan of action to get what you want out of life. Invest 60 seconds of your 86,400 seconds a day wisely. To change yourself, to change your life, it takes only 60 seconds – only ONE MIN-UTE out of any hour of any day.

Don't spend another second, minute, hour, day, month, or year of your life settling for less than you deserve. Give life all you've got. Life is not only a challenge, but an opportunity. Life is complex with its paradoxes of pain and pleasure, success and failure. You just need to search within yourself. I challenge you to get excited about life. You have 86,400 seconds every day to make a difference. Use them wisely. Spend **5 minutes** a day unlocking the miracle of motivation, the power of goals, the strength of affirmations and you will awaken The Master Motivator, The Wizard Within. The clock is ticking - go to work. **Good luck!**

*"Most of the important things in the world have been accomplished by people who have kept on trying when there seemed to be no hope at all."* - Dale Carnegie

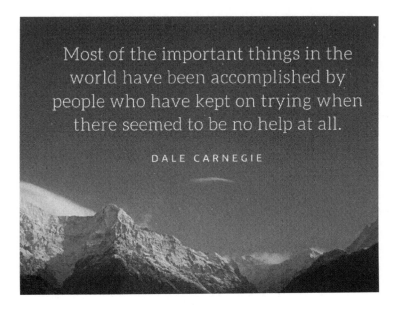

*The past is history, the future is a mystery...*

*This moment right here, right now, is a gift.*

**Which is why we call it the present.**

*O*ur goal in this book is to unwrap the gifts of your life, and make use of your present - this moment and the next "minutes." Of your life. Minutes become hours, hours become days, days become weeks, weeks become months and months become years. By implementing these "One-Minute Motivators" daily, you can turn good to great.

*Y*ou see, once you started this book you opened my time machine. Whatever happened in your past is done and over with. Don't hang on to bad memories, learn from the past and move on. You can't undo your past, so once we accept it, we are able to move on and enjoy our "present." I'm sorry if someone hurt your feelings, but dwelling on the past will not help your future. Our future can be determined by our present mindset, what we think, feel and do right here, right now is the gift of life. Nobody gets to live life backward.

**Look ahead, that is where your future lies.**

I challenge you to improve your life. The world is full of opportunities waiting to be seized and as you've seen, new ones turn up every day. The key to most of these opportunities is taking action. Action fueled by desire and complemented by energy. I challenge you to take action now. I challenge you to spend "5 minutes" every day. I challenge you to decide every day to be the best you can be. *Remember, the key is to not change the world, but to change yourself.*

 Imagine that in the Game of Life, you own a bank account that credits your account each morning with $86,400. However, it carries over no balance from day-to-day. Every evening, the bank deletes whatever part of the balance you failed to use during that day. What would you do? Draw out every cent - of course! Each of us, has such a bank account within ourselves... it's called TIME. Every morning, we receive 86,400 seconds for the day. Every night, whatever time we have failed to use is written off as a loss, and you have failed to invest. Life carries over no balance of time. And it allows no overdraft! Each day it opens a fresh new account for you.

Each evening it burns the remains of the day. If you fail to utilize your daily deposits of time, you alone are responsible for the loss.

From this MINUTE forward remember that, if you fail to utilize your daily deposits of TIME, the loss is solely yours.

There is no going back.

There is no drawing against the "tomorrow".

You must live in the present on today's deposits.

Invest it wisely so you derive the utmost in health, happiness, and success.

The clock of life is running. Make the most of today, every day. Invest your 86,400 seconds wisely and deliberately. In life you can always get more money, but time spent is lost forever.

To realize the value of **ONE YEAR**, ask a student who failed a grade and was held back.

To realize the value of **ONE MONTH**, ask a mother who gave birth to a premature baby.

To realize the value of **ONE WEEK**, ask the editor of a weekly newspaper.

To realize the value of **ONE HOUR**, ask the person holding on for his or her life.

To realize the value of **ONE MINUTE**, ask a person who missed their plane.

To realize the value of **ONE SECOND**, ask a person who just avoided an accident.

Treasure every second, every minute and every hour, of every day, for the rest of your life. Live each day as it is your last.

Imagine "One Minute" here, "One Minute" there, can change your day, your attitude and thus your life. I hope you enjoyed this book, now take "**1 Minute**" and call a friend, call a loved one, hug your child, your spouse.

Yes "**1 Minute**," 60 seconds, is a small investment from your 86,400 seconds we receive each day. So from here on in, use your time, your minutes wisely.

## *GOOD LUCK*

# EPILOGUE
## ONE-MINUTE EXERCISES

*Personal success is a result of two factors:*

*1. You must know what you really want*

*2. You must determine the price that you will pay to achieve it*

**1. Begin with your values; what are your three most important values, qualities and factors, in your life today?**

1. _____

2. _____

3. _____

**2. What would you do, how would you change your life, if you received $1,000,000 cash today?**

1. _____

2. _____

3. _____

**3. What would you do, how would you change your life if you learned today that you only had six months to live?**

1. _____

2. _____

3. _____

**4. What sort of work or activity gives you the greatest feeling of importance and personal satisfaction?**

1. _____

2. _____

3. _____

**5. What have you always wanted to do but been afraid to attempt?**

1. _____

2. _____

3. _____

**6. If you could make any significant changes in your life today, what would they be?**

1. _____

2. _____

3. _____

**7. What one great thing would you dare to dream if you knew you could not fail?**

1. _____

2. _____

3. _____

**To achieve greatly in life, you need to be clear about your goals in the seven main areas of life:**

*1. Personal*
*2. Family*
*3. Business*
*4. Financial*
*5. Education*
*6. Health*
*7. Social*

**When you set your goals, imagine you have no limitations!**

**1. List your three most intensely desired personal goals:**

   1. _____

   2. _____

   3. _____

**2. What are you three most important family and relationship goals?**

   1. _____

   2. _____

   3. _____

**3. List your three most important business and career goals?**

   1. _____

   2. _____

   3. _____

**4. What are your three most important financial goals?**

   1. _____

   2. _____

   3. _____

**5. What are your three most important educational goals, your goals for personal and professional development?**

   1. _____

   2. _____

   3. _____

6. **What are your three most important health goals - physical fitness, sports, and weight?**

   1. _____

   2. _____

   3. _____

7. **What are your three most important social goals? What contributions do you want to make to your community?**

   1. _____

   2. _____

   3. _____

8. **Without referring to your answers in the previous goal-setting question section, make a list of 10 goals you would like to accomplish in the next 12 months:**

   1. _____

   2. _____

   3. _____

   4. _____

   5. _____

   6. _____

   7. _____

   8. _____

   9. _____

   10. _____

**9. Imagine you could be absolutely guaranteed of success in any of your goals, which one goal would you choose and why?**

1. _____

2. _____

3. _____

Hopefully you spent the time to fill out the Goal sheets, now daily you must review your goals "one minute" a day and let them act as one you "**1 Minute** motivator. Spend "**1 Minute**" each day mapping out your daily program. I will never forget the scene in the Disney movie, *Alice in Wonderland*, when Alice confronts the Cheshire cat and asks, "Which road do I take?" The cat answers Alice, "Where are you going?" and Alice responds, "I don't know," to which the cat says, "Then it doesn't matter which road you take." If you don't know where you are going, then that is where you will end up. Set goals and monitor them. Setting goals is a healthy habit. Monitoring goals is a healthier habit. If you spent "**1 Minute**" per day setting goals and monitoring the goals you set, you will reach levels of health, wealth, and happiness beyond your current state. If you don't plan to succeed, then you don't have a plan for success. If you don't plan to be healthy, then you don't have a healthy plan. If you don't plan to be happy, then you might as well plan not to be happy.

We must plan our life and live our plan. When you recognize that setting goals is a healthy person habit, then you must affirm them, and again, we revisit the word "affirmation." We must say who we are, what we are, and where we are going. "I am happy, I am healthy, and I am successful." Life is for living, loving, laughing, and learning, not just for whining, worrying, or working. We need to live, we need to love, we need to laugh, and these can all be healthy habits. Remembering **1 Minute** can change one thought, motivate one person so use your minutes wisely

**Let's** work hard and do it today.

**Let's** live in the moment.

**Let's** set goals today. Let's recite our affirmations today.

**Let's** take responsibility for our lives today.

**Let's** never quit.

**Let's** commit ourselves to overcome any and all adversities in our life.

**Let's** network more and complain less.

**Let's** dedicate ourselves to developing a winning belief system.

**Let's** develop an attitude that will carry us to the top.

Remember, there's no better time than now and no better place then here, now, today. Affirm to develop the traits of success and allow your Inner Winner to work. Spend the next "**1 Minute**" stretching your mind, setting goals, studying, and committing to my traits for your success. And if you feel "**1 Minute**" is not enough, get my book *The 5 Minute Motivator*.

Let's start work hard and do it this minute. Give yourself 60 Seconds to begin your transformation. Study these goals you have written, review them often, it'll only take a minute.

Let's live in the moment. Let's set "**1 Minute**" goals today and everyday. Let's recite our **1 Minute** affirmations today. Let's take responsibility for our lives today. Let's never quit. Let's commit ourselves to overcome any and all adversities in our life. Let's network more and complain less. Let's dedicate ourselves to developing a winning belief system. Let's develop an attitude that will carry us to the top. Remember, there's no better time than now and no better place then here, now, today. Affirm to develop the traits of success and allow your Inner Winner to work. Spend 1minutes each hour of each day stretching your mind, setting goals, studying, and committing to your success.

In closing remember, that time, not money, is life's most valuable commodity. Live a life with no regrets and give thanks to your friends and family because they shared their time and their life with you. They believed you were someone special enough to spend their lives with you. Remember that time waits for no one. Life is not only a challenge, but an opportunity. Life is complex with its paradoxes of pain and pleasure, success and failure. You just need to search within yourself. I challenge you to get excited about life. You have 86,400 seconds every day to make a difference. Use them wisely. Spend **"1 Minute"** a day unlocking the miracle of motivation, the power of goals, the strength of affirmations and you will awaken, "The Winner Within."

THE CLOCK IS STILL TICKING

NOW GO TO WORK.

FOLLOW YOUR PASSION, IT KNOWS WHERE YOU SHOULD GO.

HELP PEOPLE. **EXPLORE, PLAY, LAUGH, ENJOY.**

**MOVE MORE, STRESS LESS. SET AND CELEBRATE MILESTONES.**

YOU HAVE TO PUT SOMETHING OUT THERE TO GET SOMETHING BACK.

EVERYTHING YOU WANT AND NEED IS UP TO YOU TO MAKE HAPPEN. MAKE YOUR OWN PATH.

**CARVE A NICHE, GET IT OUT THERE.**

**DEFINE WHAT SUCCESS LOOKS LIKE TO YOU, THEN GO AFTER IT.**

**DO IT NOW.** COLLECT EXPERIENCES NOT THINGS.

*IGNORE DOUBTERS, EVEN WHEN THEY ARE WITHIN YOUR OWN HEAD.*

**BELIEVE IN YOURSELF. NOURISH YOUR MIND AND BODY, TAKE TIME OUT OFTEN.**

**GIVE YOURSELF PERMISSION.**

**BE YOUR OWN HERO.** *TRUST YOUR INSTINCTS, TAKE IT ONE STEP AT A TIME.*

BUILD YOUR DAYS AROUND WHAT IS IMPORTANT TO YOU.

**WHEN YOU ARE DOING WHAT IS PASSIONATE FOR YOU, YOU ARE MAKING THE WORLD A BETTER PLACE.**

**NEVER STOP LEARNING AND EXPERIMENTING.**

**THE LESS YOU SPEND THE MORE YOU HAVE. BE THANKFUL, BE HUMBLE.**

DO NOT BE AFRAID TO REVISIT YOUR GOALS. SIMPLICITY IS KEY! ⚷ ⚷

Made in the USA
Columbia, SC
08 August 2020

14737475R00102